View of the Action
of the Federal Government
in Behalf of Slavery

VIEW OF THE ACTION

OF THE

FEDERAL GOVERNMENT,

IN

BEHALF OF SLAVERY.

BY WILLIAM JAY.

"We, THE PEOPLE OF THE UNITED STATES, do ordain and establish this Constitution."—*Federal Constitution.*

SECOND EDITION.

NEW YORK:

PUBLISHED BY

THE AMERICAN ANTI-SLAVERY SOCIEY,

No. 143 NASSAU STREET.

1839

Engraved by Geo. E. Perine, New York
after the Painting by Wenzler, in the Court House at White Plains, N.Y.
Courtesy of New York Public Library, Picture Collection

William Jay

WILLIAM JAY

View
of the Action
of the Federal
Government
in Behalf of
Slavery

BERGMAN PUBLISHERS
New York

First published: New York, 1839

—————

Published, 1969, by
BERGMAN PUBLISHERS
224 West Twentieth Street
New York, N.Y. 10011

This edition has been reproduced in its entirety from an
original copy in the New York Public Library

—————

Standard Book Number: 87503-018-1

Library of Congress Catalog Card Number: 68-59224

—————

Printed in the United States of America

CONTENTS.

1*

INTRODUCTION.

THE rapid sale of the first edition of this work, and the almost immediate call for another, afford gratifying evidence of
the awakening attention of the public, to the action of the Federal government in behalf of slavery. That action is so iniquitous
in itself, and so dangerous in its consequences to the liberties of
the country, that it needs only to be fully known, to be restrained by the patriotism and moral sense of the community, within
the limits prescribed by the constitution, and the obvious principles of humanity and justice. It is not easy, however, to enlighten those who prefer darkness to light ; nor to persuade men
to act in opposition to their supposed pecuniary or political interests. But there can be no triumph, where there is no struggle—that religion is worthless, which co-operates with human
depravity ; and that patriotism an empty name, which only
echoes the shout of the multitude.

If the friends of human liberty, have in this country much to
cover them with grief and shame ; they have also much to stimulate their exertions ; and much to assure them of ultimate
success. Their own rights—the virtue, happiness and liberty
of their descendants—the honor, prosperity and freedom of their
country, are all involved in the issue. Slavery is a perfidious,
encroaching enemy, that must either conquer or be conquered.
Let the warfare now waged against it, be succeeded by a peace,
and soon Texas, the Valley of the Mississippi, and in time even the
Atlantic states would be added to its dominions. Every dictate,
therefore, of patriotism or religion, of personal interest, of pater-
nal affection, unite in urging us to use all lawful means to stay the

progress of the destroyer, and to teach our children after us, to continue the contest.

But is not the struggle hopeless, and ought we not to sit down in utter despair at the prospect of desolation, misery and disgrace with which our country is threatened ?   So we are advised by high authority—PUBLIC OPINION, we are told, is against us. Indeed! and is it not also against every defeated candidate for office, and every losing political party ? But who hears our baffled politicians advising submission to the victors because public opinion is against the vanquished ?   Public opinion is a mighty agent for good or for evil ; but it is as fickle as it is powerful. It strewed the path of the Redeemer with palm branches, and afterwards nailed him to the cross.

For ages it guarded and preserved all the oppressions and cruelties of the feudal system—it is now gradually, but surely destroying its every vestige. But a few years since, public opinion, not merely sanctioned, but actually required the use of intoxicating liquors—it is now, their potent enemy.

But perhaps the most extraordinary change this mighty agent has undergone, is in relation to slavery itself ; and the friends of emancipation will find in the history of this transformation, one of their most powerful inducements to perseverance.

For more than two hundred years before its abolition, had the African slave trade been pursued by Christian nations, under the fostering protection of their rulers. No difference of religious faith, of government, or of climate, offered any check to this accursed commerce. Catholics and Protestants, the subjects of Monarchs and the citizens of Republics, natives of the north and of the south, alike thirsted for the price of blood, alike participated in robbery and murder. In 1774, the British cabinet refused its assent to the imposition by the colonial legislatures of duties on the importation of slaves. " We cannot," said the Secretary, Lord Dartmouth, " allow the colonies to check or discourage in *any degree* a traffic so beneficial to the nation "! !

The feelings of humanity and the powers of conscience, were on this subject almost universally and totally paralyzed. So late as 1783, in the trial of a civil cause in London, it appeared in evidence, that one hundred and thirty-two Africans had been thrown into the sea by the captain of a slaver to defraud the underwriters. Minutes of the evidence were submitted to the government; but the victims were only *negroes*, and their murderer was unmolested.

In 1786, the number of unhappy beings annually torn from Africa, was estimated at 100,000. Of these, it was admitted at least 20,000 perished on the voyage; and of those who survived to enter a state of hopeless bondage, 20,000 more, exhausted by suffering and despair, sunk into the grave within two years.

Individuals were occasionally found who protested against the traffic, but their voices were unheeded. For two centuries not a word in reprobation of the trade had been uttered within the walls of the British senate. This long silence was first broken by Mr. David Hartley, who in 1776, moved in the House of Commons, that the slave trade was "contrary to the laws of God and the rights of man." But the moral sense of Great Britain, and indeed of the world, was then too obtuse to recognise these simple and now obvious truths; and the resolution was promptly rejected. Seven years after, a petition against the trade, the first ever offered, was presented by the Quaker Society to the House of Commons. But that body did not even condescend to consider it—the Premier, Lord North, coolly observing, that the traffic had, in a commercial view, become *necessary* to almost every nation in Europe.

On the 7th July, 1783, shortly after this official declaration, SIX Quakers* met in London "to consider what steps they should take for THE RELIEF AND LIBERATION OF THE NEGRO SLAVES IN THE WEST INDIES, *and* FOR THE DISCOURAGEMENT OF THE SLAVE TRADE ON THE COAST OF AFRICA."

When we reflect on the peculiar circumstances under which these men assembled, we cannot but regard their meeting as one of the sublimest instances of Christian faith unrecorded in the sa-

* William Dillwyn, George Harrison, Samuel Hoare, Thomas Knowles, John Lloyd, and Joseph Woods. Their names are re gistered in heaven, let them not be forgotten on earth.

cred volume—a faith which, according to the promise, was effectual in removing mountains. At the moment of their meeting, the
maritime powers of Europe were actively engaged in the trade
—a trade against which no petition had ever been presented
except from the very sect to which they belonged, and which
had within a few days, like certain petitions in modern times,
been ordered to " *lie on the table.*" They had, moreover, just
witnessed the impunity of the wretch who had deliberately
drowned one hundred and thirty-two of his fellow men—an impunity which warned them of the utter insensibility of the public to the sufferings of the miserable negroes.

And who were these six men, who under such circumstances
presumed to attempt the abolition of slavery and the slave trade
—who aspired to move the moral world—to arrest the commerce of nations—to proclaim liberty to the captive, and the
opening of the prison doors to them that were bound ? Did they
sway the councils, or lead the armies of Empires—were they
possessed of learning to command the attention of the wise and
great ; or of eloquence to mould at their will the passions of
multitudes ? They were humble and obscure individuals, belonging to a small and despised sect, and precluded by their
religious tenets and social condition from all political influence.
But they had discovered from the Book of God, what had
escaped many wise and good men, that the trade in question
was opposed alike to the attributes and the precepts of the
Almighty Ruler of nations.

In laboring, therefore, for its suppression, they were assured of his approbation ; and without regarding their own
weakness, or the obstacles before them, they proceeded steadily
in the path of duty, leaving the result to HIM with whom all
things are possible.

They determined to hold frequent meetings, of which regular
minutes were kept. Their first object was to enlighten and
purify the public mind, and for this purpose they entered into
negotiations with the proprietors of various newspapers, and secured a space in their columns for such articles respecting the
trade as they might choose to insert. They likewise circulated

books and pamphlets on the subject. The seeds thus scattered germinated slowly, but ultimately yielded a glorious harvest. Within two years a second petition was presented, and like the first was treated with neglect. The third year, the six associates, with the aid of some friends, engaged the celebrated Clarkson as their agent; and so successful were his labors in exciting the sensibilities of the British public, that it was found expedient to divest the enterprize of its sectarian character, and the committee added six to their number from other denominations. This new committee soon became an important body, receiving and appropriating the pecuniary contributions to the cause, and directing and cheering the labors of its advocates. Gradually, members of Parliament, dignitaries of the church, and political leaders subscribed to the funds of the committee, and avowed their hostility to the trade.

Petitions were multiplied, and the government so far condescended to notice the rising excitement, as to appoint a commission to inquire into the alleged atrocities of this branch of the British commerce. On the 9th of May, 1788, only five years after the first meeting of the Committee, the House of Commons voted that they would at the next session take into consideration the complaints against the African slave trade.

It is unnecessary for our purpose to pursue the details of this instructive history. It has already taught us the possibility of rousing the public attention however lethargic, by appeals to the conscience and understanding; and the influence which Christian zeal and faith, unaided by wealth and power, are capable of exerting. The few remaining facts we shall notice, convey the important lesson, that no cause, however pure, no truth however obvious, can shield their advocates from obloquy, when prejudice and selfishness find it expedient to assail them; and also, that constancy in maintaining and inculcating the great principles of justice and humanity will finally be crowned with success.

No sooner did a parliamentary inquiry threaten to expose the abominations and endanger the continuance of the traffic, than its advocates, reckless alike of truth and decency, vindicated its policy, and attacked with vindictive fury those who were labor-

2

ing to destroy it. Abolition was denounced in parliament as " hypocritical, fanatic, and methodistical." It would lead, it was asserted, to " insurrection, massacre and ruin in the Colonies ; and in Great Britain to the reduction of her revenue, the decay of her naval strength, and the bankruptcy of her merchants and manufactures." The trade was justified by the press ; and even ministers of religion stepped forth to vindicate it on Scriptural authority.* In 1791, a bill was brought in for the suppression of the trade. The opposition to it was malignant and success- ful. The measure was pronounced fit only for the bigotry of the 12th century. Lord John Russell termed it " visionary and delusive ; a feeble attempt to serve the cause of humanity, as other nations would pursue the trade if abolished by Great Britain. Mr. Stanley insisted that it was the intention of Pro- vidence, from the beginning, *that one set of men should be slaves to another;* and he complained that the trade had been con- demned from the pulpit !

The friends of abolition were ridiculed by Lord Chancellor Thurlow from the woolsack ; and the Duke of Clarence, who afterwards, as WILLIAM THE FOURTH, gave his assent to the bill abolishing slavery throughout his dominions, regardless of par- liamentary decorum, declared, in his place in the House of Lords, that the abolitionists were hypocrites and fanatics ; and in the application of these epithets included Mr. Wilberforce by name.

Ten times did Mr. Wilberforce, in the House of Commons, endeavor to procure the suppression of the traffic, and ten times was he doomed to defeat. So late as 1807, Lord Castlereagh, in the British senate, vindicated the trade on scriptural grounds, and avowed that, in his opinion, the advantages resulting from it were so great, that were it not now existing, the trade ought

* As illustrative of public opinion at this time, we give the titles of two pamphlets published in London in 1788, viz. " Slavery no Oppression," and " Scriptural Researches on the Licitness of the Slave Trade, and showing its conformity with the principles of natural and revealed religion, delineated in the writings of the word of God." *By the Rev. R. Harris.*

forthwith to be established. But the triumph of justice, and the reward of faith and perseverance were nigh at hand. On the 25th March, 1807, twenty-four years after the formation of the Quaker Committee, the slave trade was abolished by act of Parliament.

Splendid and glorious as was this triumph, it was incomplete while shared by Great Britain alone. The whole of Christendom was yet to be brought to abjure a commerce condemned alike by reason and revelation. A long course of negotiation ensued, and treaty after treaty was made for the abandonment of the traffic, until, in 1830, every Christian nation in Europe and America had prohibited it.

The Quaker Committee, as we have seen, proposed, in 1783, not merely the discouragement of the African slave trade, but also " the liberation of negro slaves in the West Indies." The struggle for this last object was continued after the accomplishment of the former for thirty-one years ; when, on the 4th Aug. 1838, negro slavery wholly ceased throughout the British West Indies, and every legal disability, founded on color, was utterly abolished.

Thus has been accomplished the most astonishing revolution in opinion and practice the world has ever witnessed, with the exception of the establishment of Christianity. And let it be remembered, that this revolution was effected solely by the exhibition of truth, and by bold and persevering appeals to the conscience and understanding of mankind. No miracles have wrought conviction, no force has subdued opposition. Public opinion was gradually enlightened and converted, and then roused into action, and with resistless energy it smote to the earth a stupendous system of wickedness and cruelty.

Surely we may learn from this history a very different lesson from that which many of our politicians and moralists are fond of inculcating—that because public opinion is against them, *therefore* abolitionists should cease to do well, and learn to do evil—should abandon their opposition to slavery and acquiesce in popular iniquity. Let us take the six Quakers for our example, and resolve to persevere while life shall be spared in our assaults upon slavery, not inquiring how many are against us, knowing assuredly that God is for us. But should the advocates of emancipation, in some moment of weakness or of trial, be tempted to cast a desponding and inquiring glance over the field of battle, and to recall to his recollection the events of the campaign, he will see nothing in the array of hostile forces to damp his courage, nor in the review of the past to lower his confidence of victory.

The great object proposed by the friends of human liberty, so far as relates to the Federal Government, is the abolition of slavery within its " exclusive jurisdiction." But we have been given to understand,* that " the immediate abolition of slavery in the District of Columbia is utterly impracticable." That the *present* administration do not *choose* to abolish it, is not more true than that the British Parliament of 1783 did not choose to abolish the slave trade ; and it is equally true that the abolition of slavery in the District of Columbia is now far more probable and practicable than was that of the slave trade and West India slavery at the formation of the Quaker Committee. But why is the immediate abolition of slavery in the District utterly impracticable ? " Because public opinion throughout the Union is against it." This is a good reason for predicting that the next Congress will not grant abolition, but not why the friends of abolition should cease their efforts to change public opinion, in order that a future Congress may grant what we know the next will refuse.

In many respects the abolitionists of the present day are placed in circumstances similar to those in which their predecessors found themselves in 1783. They, like us, had to contend with the hostility of the Government, with the interests and prejudices of slaveholders in the legislature† ; with clerical defenders of cruelty and oppression , with mercantile-cupidity, and with heart-

* Public letter of John Quincy Adams of 25th May, 1839.

† Many of the Commoners and Lords were deeply interested in West Indian plantations ; and a large estate, well stocked with slaves, was held by a chartered Society of the established Church.

less politicians. But in many other respects they were less favored than we are. They were struggling *against* the spirit of the age, we are co-operating with it. They were advancing untried theories—we can point to the West Indies and South America for the practical and successful operation of our doctrines. They were striving to influence a Government in a great degree independent of the people—we are petitioning a Government that is the mere creature of the popular will. They were few and despised—the hatred and persecution we have experienced attest the importance attributed to us. They were without political influence—where suffrage is universal 300,000 petitioners will not be overlooked by politicians. They could bring their facts and arguments before the public only by hiring a space in the columns of a few newspapers—we have numerous periodicals, many of them of the largest size, exclusively devoted to the propagation of our opinions, while many religious and political journals are aiding us in exhibiting the evils of slavery and the advantages of emancipation. They were cheered by no official sanction of their efforts—we are encouraged and stimulated, in many instances, by the approving voice of the representatives of the people.

We ask Congress to abolish slavery in the District; is the prayer presumptuous or unconstitutional? If so, it becomes not the House of Representatives to rebuke us; for, on the 9th Jan. 1829, that body " Resolved that the Committee on the District of Columbia be instructed to inquire into the expediency of providing *by law* for the gradual abolition of slavery within the District, in such manner that the interests of no individual shall be injured thereby." Here we have the solemn admission of the popular and most numerous branch of the legislature, that the question of abolition is one of *expediency* alone, and not of constitutional power; and that slavery may be terminated by law, without injury to any individual. And what sentiments on this subject have been uttered by the State Legislatures? In 1828 the Legislature of PENNSYLVANIA instructed their members of Congress " to procure, if practicable, the passage of a law to abolish slavery in the District of Columbia." In 1829, the As-
2*

sembly of NEW YORK voted to direct the representatives from
that state " to make every proper exertion to effect the passage of a law for the abolition of slavery in the District of
of Columbia." In 1837, the Senate of MASSACHUSETTS " Resolved that Congress, having exclusive legislation in the District
of Columbia, possess the right to abolish slavery and the slave
trade therein, and that the early exercise of such right is demanded by the enlightened sentiment of the civilized world, by
the principles of the revolution, and by humanity." The other
House, the same session, " Resolved that Congress, having exclusive legislation in the District of Columbia, possess the right
to abolish slavery in said District, and that its exercise should
only be restrained by a regard to the public good." The next
session both branches of the legislature resolved " That the
rights of justice, the claims of humanity, and the common good
alike demand the entire suppression of the slave trade now carried on in the District of Columbia." In 1838 the House of
Representatives of the Legislature of MAINE " Resolved that
the continuance of slavery within the sacred enclosure and
chosen seat of the National Government is inconsistent with a
due regard to the enlightened judgment of mankind, and with
all just pretensions on our part to the character of a free people,
and is adapted to bring into contempt republican liberty, and
render its influence powerless throughout the world." The
same year the Legislature of VERMONT, without a dissenting
voice, instructed the representatives in Congress " to use their
utmost efforts to procure the abolition of slavery and the slave
trade in the District of Columbia." Yet there are those who
would fain paralyze all our efforts by the assurance that public
opinion is against us !

But we are urged to desist, not only because our object is
impracticable, but also because it is *unlawful.* " When the
people," we are told, "are bound by laws emanating from a
legislative assembly wherein they have no representatives, *their
will* must be ascertained by manifestations from themselves."
But why ought Congress to ascertain the will of the people of the
District ? Because " the Declaration of Independence derives

all just powers of the Government from the consent of the governed." But are laws binding only on such as approve of
them? No—" When the people are represented in the legislative assembly, the *consent of the whole* must be inferred from
the voice of the representative majority." Now it so happens
that the whole people of the United States, by the voice of the
representative majority, assented to the provision of the Constitution, that a district, ten miles square, should be placed under
the absolute and exclusive jurisdiction of Congress. To this arrangement the people inhabiting the present District gave their
assent through their representatives. Afterwards, when they
themselves were set off, by the legislatures of Virginia and
Maryland, to be the subjects of this exclusive jurisdiction, they,
through their representatives in the legislatures, consented to
be thus placed under the authority of Congress. And shall we
now be gravely told, after these people have thus consented to
be governed, in all cases whatsoever, by the National Legislature, and after the people of the United States have, for this
purpose, vested unlimited and exclusive jurisdiction in Congress,
that it is contrary to the principles of the Declaration of Independence that this jurisdiction should secure to each inhabitant
of the District the "inalienable rights of life, liberty, and the
pursuit of happiness!" Again, if the Declaration derives the
powers of the government from the consent of the governed,
from what representative majority, we would ask, are we to infer the *consent* of six thousand of the people of the District to be
reduced to chattels—to be robbed of the rights of humanity—to
be converted, with their wives and children, into articles of
merchandise?

Surely the friends of emancipation will not, after their past
experience, look upon public opinion as an *invincible* enemy—
still less will they believe that the Declaration of Independence
is the death-warrant of human rights in the national domain.
The principles for which they are contending are the principles
of the Declaration—the means they are using are those given
them by the Constitution—freedom of speech and of the press—
petition and the elective franchise; and, by the blessing of God

on these principles and means, they will yet convert public opinion into an ally—will yet purge the capital of the Republic of its loathsome plague, and restore the Federal Government to its legitimate functions, of establishing justice and securing the blessings of liberty.

Bedford, September, 1839.

A

VIEW OF THE ACTION

OF THE

GENERAL GOVERMENT.

———

OUR Fathers, in forming the Federal Constitution, entered into a guilty compromise on the subject of Slavery, and heavily is their sin now visited upon their children. By that instrument, the continuance of the African slave-trade was guaranteed for twenty years;—a larger proportional representation in Congress, and a larger vote in the election of the Executive, was accorded to the slave-holding, than to the other States:—the power of the nation was pledged to keep the slave in subjection; and should he ever escape from his fetters, his master was authorised to pursue and to seize him, in any and every of the sovereign States composing our wide-spread confederacy.

We are not about to exhibit the corrupting influence of this compact on the religious sympathies and sentiments of our countrymen, in regard to slavery; nor is it our present purpose to trace the retributive justice of Heaven in that recklessness of human life, and in that contempt of human and divine obligations which are hurrying on the slave States to anarchy and barbarism; or in the eagerness so generally exhibited by our northern politicians and merchants, to barter the constitutional rights of themselves and their fellow-citizens, for the votes and the trade of the South.*

We propose simply to take a view of the action of the Federal Government in behalf of slavery,—a subject that has yet been but partially investigated; and we flatter ourselves, that in the course of our inquiries, we shall develope facts, which, with some at least of our readers, will possess the merit of novelty. These facts, for the most part, derive their origin from

---

* Before this language is condemned as harsh and exaggerated, we beg the reader to recall some of the prominent events of the last few years, connected with this subject :—the Lynch clubs and cruel inflictions of the South—the sacking of the Charleston post-office—the wholesale and unpunished murders at Vicksburg, —and the frequent burnings alive of negroes, and in particular of McIntosh, taken by the citizens of St. Louis from the prison, chained to a tree, and consumed by a slow fire—and the advice of Judge Lawless to the Grand Jury, not to notice the diabolical atrocity, because it was, in fact, the act of the community! As to the North, we point in our justification to the innumerable mobs excited by politicians against the friends of emancipation—the various attempts made by the state authorities to propitiate the South, by a surrender of the freedom of speech, and of the press— to the zeal of the merchants in our seaports in getting up anti-abolition meetings—to the conflagration of Pennsylvania Hall, and to the martyrdom of Lovejoy. In truth, our whole land is strewed with monuments of the wickedness and tyranny of slavery —monuments which declare, in no doubtful language, that our common national sin is not unheeded by HIM to whom vengeance belongeth.

THE FEDERAL RATIO OF REPRESENTATION.

The Constitution provides that the members of the Lower House of Congress shall be proportioned to the free inhabitants of the States they represent, *except* that in each State three-fifths of the slave population shall be for this purpose considered as free inhabitants. In other words, every five slaves are to be counted as three white persons. For example, if by law every 60,000 free inhabitants may elect a representative, a district containing 45,000 whites and 25,000 slaves, becomes by the *federal ratio* entitled to a member. This stipulation in the Constitution has from the beginning given the slaveholders an undue weight in the national councils. A few instances will illustrate its practical effect. The whole number of the House of Representatives is at present 242—sent from 26 States. Of these, the following are *slave* States, viz.:—Delaware, Maryland, Virginia, North Carolina, South Carolina, Georgia, Kentucky, Tennessee, Alabama, Mississippi, Louisiana, Missouri, and Arkansas. These States, with a free population of 3,823,389, have 100 members; while the *free* States, with a free population nearly double, viz. 7,003,451, have only 142 members. One representative is at present allowed to 47,700 inhabitants. Now, were the slaves omitted in the enumeration, the slave States would have only 75 members. Hence it follows, that at the present moment, the slaveholding interest has a representation of TWENTY-FIVE members in *addition* to the fair and equal representation of the free inhabitants. There is certainly no good reason why the owners of human chattels, should, by the fundamental law of a *Republic*, have greater privileges awarded to them than to the holders of any other kind of property whatever. But such is the compact; we seek not to change or violate it, but only to explain its operation.

Each State has as many votes for President as it has members of Congress. The rule of representation in the Lower House has already been explained; in the Senate it is different: and *each* State, whatever be its population, has two Senators, and no more. The free population of the slave States, as already stated, is *half* that of the others; but their *number* being equal, their representation in the Senate is also equal.

If free population were the principle of representation in the Federal Government, as it is with scarcely an exception in all the States, the slave States would have

In the Senate,	13 members.
In the House,	75
Electoral votes for President,	88
They *have*, In the Senate,	26 members.
In the House,	100
Electoral votes for President,	126

Here we find the secret of the power of the South, and of the obsequiousness of the North. Ohio, with a population of 947,000, has 19 members; while Virginia, with a free population of 200,000 LESS, has *two* members MORE. Take another example. Pennsylvania has 30 electoral votes; the States of South Carolina, Georgia, Alabama, Mississippi, Louisiana, and Kentucky, with an *aggregate* free population of 189,791 *less* than Pennsylvania, have 53 electoral votes!

It cannot be supposed that this vast and most unequal representation and consequent political power, will be unemployed by its possessors. On the contrary, the slaveholders in Congress have uniformly succeeded in effecting their objects, when united among themselevs. In 1836, this slave power in Congress was adroitly turned to pecuniary profit. The Surplus Revenue remaining in the Treasury on the 1st of January, 1837, was to be distributed, and the rule of distribution became a question. The income, it is true, had been derived chiefly from the industry and enterprise of the North; but the South insisted, and with her usual success, that instead of dividing the money according to population, it should be apportioned among the States according to their *electoral votes*. By this rule, the slave States, notwithstanding their inferiority in population, would share alike with the free, so far as regarded the number of their Senators; and with regard to their representatives, they would secure an apportionment of money on account of three-fifths of their two millions of slaves.

The sum allotted by this gross and monstrous rule to the States of South Carolina, Georgia, Alabama, Mississippi, Louisiana, and Kentucky, was $6,754,588; while Pennsylvania, with a free population *larger* than

3

that of all these six States together, was to receive only $3,823,353 ; so that, in fact, the slaveholders of these States received, man for man, just about twice as many dollars from the national treasury as the hard-working citizens of Pennsylvania!

Notwithstanding this slave representation, the free States have a majority of members; and hence it becomes important to investigate

THE SOURCES OF THE SLAVEHOLDING INFLUENCE IN CONGRESS.

These may be regarded as threefold: first, their anxiety to protect and perpetuate slavery, renders the southern members united in whatever measures they consider important for this purpose, while the representatives from the North, having no common bond of union, are divided in opinion and effort. Secondly, a slave State having more votes to bestow on a presidential candidate, and more members in Congress to support or oppose the administration than a free State of equal white population, is of course of greater consequence in the estimation of politicians; and hence arises an influence reaching to every measure, and weighing upon every question. Thirdly, the peculiar temperament of the southern gentlemen, together with their observation of the servility of the northern politicians, have induced them to resort, and with great success, to INTIMIDATION as a means of influence.

The practice adopted by the slaveholders of threatening on all occasions to dissolve the Union, unless they are permitted to govern it, has been too long and firmly established to need illustration. We will at present merely give a few recent instances of outrageous menaces; and to justify what we have said of the servility of northern politicians, it is sufficient to observe, that these menaces were unrebuked.

On the 18th of April, 1836, a petition against the continuance of slavery in the District of Columbia was presented to the House of Representatives, when Mr. SPEIGHT, of North Carolina, declared in his place, that "he had great respect for the chair as an officer of the House, and a great respect for him personally; and *nothing but that respect* prevented him from rushing to the table and *tearing that petition to pieces.*" Of course it was to be understood, that the order of the house and the rights of northern petitioners were respected, not from any constitutional obligations, but solely because the speaker, himself a slaveholder, was acceptable to southern gentlemen.

Mr. HAMMOND, of South Carolina, the same session, in a speech, used the following language: "I warn the abolitionists, ignorant, infatuated barbarians as they are, that if chance shall throw any of them into *our hands*, he may expect a *felon's death.*"

Mr. LUMPKIN remarked in the Senate, (January, 1838,) "If abolitionists went to Georgia, they would be *caught;*" and Mr. PRESTON declared in the same debate—"Let an abolitionist come within the borders of South Carolina, if we can catch him, we will try him, and notwithstanding all the interference of all the governments on earth, including the Federal Government, we will HANG him."*

* Yet this Carolina Senator, who is thus ready to sanction

3

It seems probable from these declarations that
abolitionists, in their southern travels, will meet
with "barbarians" quite as "ignorant and infatuated" as themselves ; and also that the gibbet is to be
the fate of any member of Congress, who shall by
his votes or speeches dare to identify himself with
the abolitionists, and afterwards enter the slave
region.

Such are the sources of the slaveholding influence in Congress. The following pages will exhibit many of the results of this influence, and the
first to which the reader's attention is called, is

THE OBSEQUIOUSNESS OF THE PRESIDENTIAL CANDIDATES.

As slaveholders are ready to hang abolitionists
when they can "catch" them, it is not to be supposed that they will elect any of the proscribed sect
President of the United States. Of course, it becomes important for such gentlemen as aspire to that
honor, that their ideas on the subject of human
rights, should be adapted to the meridian of the slave
region.

Previous to the last presidential canvass, Mr.
Van Buren being a candidate, thought it prudent to
write a letter for publication, containing the following passage :—" I prefer that not only you, but all

wholesale murder for opinion's sake, in defiance "of all the governments on earth," and the government in heaven, too, has
been nominated for the office of Vice-President of the United
States, by the Whig party, in the State of Ohio, a party profess-
ing great attachment to the cause of *constitutional* liberty !

the people of the United States, shall now understand, that if the desire of that portion of them which is favorable to my election to the chief magistracy should be gratified, I must go into the presidential chair *the inflexible and uncompromising opponent* of any attempt on the part of Congress to abolish slavery in the District of Columbia, *against the wishes of the slaveholding States.*

Mr. WHITE was a rival candidate, and deemed it expedient to give his pledge also, which he did in these terms :—" I do not believe Congress has the power to abolish slavery in the District of Columbia ; and if that body did possess the power, I think the exercise of it would be the *very worst policy.* Holding these opinions, I would act on them in any situation in which I could be placed, and for both reasons would, if called on to act, *withhold my assent to any bill having in view such an object.*"

GENERAL HARRISON, a third candidate, also, as we have understood, wrote his letter, but not having it before us cannot quote it. We presume, however, it was thought sufficient, since an address in his behalf from his political friends in Virginia, assured the public that " *he is sound to the core on the subject of slavery.*"

Mr. WEBSTER, the fourth and last candidate, had many years before fully committed himself as to the power of Congress over slavery in the District. He gave no pledge, and received no vote from any slave State.

Another presidential election is approaching, and Mr. CLAY is announced as the opposing candidate to the present incumbent. This gentleman's position

with regard to human rights, has been deemed at the
South equivocal and unsatisfactory. It is true he is
a slaveholder, and although for more than twenty
years an officer, and now the President of the Colonization Society, he has refrained from availing himself of the opportunities he has possessed of manu-
mitting his slaves, and permitting them to enjoy in
Africa, the liberty which he insists it would be dangerous to allow them in America. Still his *language*
and *professions*, in relation to the " delicate subject,"
have been indiscreet. In 1827, he maintained in a
public speech the right and policy of the Federal
Government to aid the Colonization Society, and insisted that the annual increase of the colored population, bond and free, namely, 52,000, might be transported to Africa. " If," said the orator, " I could be
instrumental in eradicating this deepest stain (slavery)
upon the character of our country, and removing all
cause for reproach on account of it by foreign nations—if I could only be instrumental in ridding,
of this foul blot, that revered State (Virginia) that
gave me birth—or that not less beloved State (Kentucky) which kindly adopted me as her son, I would
not exchange the proud satisfaction which I should
enjoy for all the honor of all the triumphs ever decreed to the most successful conqueror."* In the
same speech he remarked, in reference to such as
objected to the agitation of the slavery question, " If
they would repress all tendencies towards liberty
and ultimate emancipation, they must do more than

* Speech before the American Colonization Society.—10 Rep.
p. 12.

put down the benevolent efforts of this Society. They must go back to the era of our liberty and in pendence, and muzzle the cannon which thunders its annual joyous return. They must revive the slave trade, with all its train of atrocities. They must suppress the workings of British philanthropy, seek- ing to meliorate the condition of the unfortunate West India Slaves. They must arrest the career of South American deliverance from thraldom. They must blow out the moral lights around us, and ex- tinguish the greatest torch of all which America presents to a benighted world, pointing the way to their rights, their liberties, and their happiness. They must penetrate the human soul, and eradicate the light of reason and the love of liberty. Then, and not till then, *when universal darkness and despair prevail, can you* PERPETUATE SLAVERY, *and repress all sympathies and all humane and benevolent efforts among freemen, in be- half of the unhappy portions of our race who are doomed to bondage.*"

It is not surprising that such sentiments, should ex- cite distrust of Mr. Clay at the South ; a distrust by no means likely to be dissipated by the following ex- tract from " The Life of the Hon. Henry Clay, by George G. Prentiss," published some years since— an extract which has been zealously circulated of late by southern papers, devoted to the support of *north- ern men with southern principles.* " The commence- ment of Mr. CLAY's political career may be dated as far back as the year 1797—a period at which he had scarcely begun the practice of law. The people. of Kentucky were then about to elect a convention to frame a new constitution for the State. And one

feature of the plan which had been submitted to them
was a provision for the *final emancipation of the slave
population.* The strongest prejudices of a majority of
the people, in every part of the state were arraigned
against this measure, and MR. CLAY was aware of
the fact, his SENTIMENTS and his FEELINGS
were on the side of EMANCIPATION ; and without
taking a moment's heed to his popularity, he entered
into the defence of his FAVORITE POLICY, with all
the deep and unquenchable ardor of his nature. His
vigorous pen was busy in the public journals, and his
eloquent voice was raised in almost every assemblage
in favor of the election of men to the convention who
would contend for the ERADICATION OF SLA-
VERY. A conviction of the expediency and necessity of EMANCIPATION has been spreading farther
and farther among our countrymen, and taking deeper
and deeper root in their minds, and it requires not
the spirit of prophecy to foretell the END. This rapid and continued triumph of the PRINCIPLES, of
which it was the object of MR. CLAY'S first political labors to establish, may well be a source of pride
to him and honest exultation to his friends."

Mr. Clay's course in Congress, had, moreover, not
been satisfactory to the slave party. He had not advocated the annexation of Texas—he had not denied
the constitutional power of Congress to abolish slavery in the District—he had expressed himself in
favor of receiving abolition petitions—and, above all,
he had voted against Mr. Calhoun's bill establishing a
censorship of the press ; a bill which received the
sanction of Mr. Van Buren, and his partizans, the two
New York Senators, Messrs. Wright and Tallmadge.

The administration party at the South, were making great use of all these circumstances against Mr. Clay, and it became obvious that unless he could conciliate the slaveholders, he had little prospect of success.

The Mobile " Commercial Register" thus announced the demand of the South.

" We must do by Mr. Clay as the South have done by Mr. Van Buren—leave him not an inch of neutral ground to stand upon between the South and the fanatics. *We must push him as far as Mr. Van Buren was pushed.* The southern safety demands it. *He must measure the whole length,* and walk altogether off the middle neutral ground which he occupies, OR THE SOUTH WILL REJECT AND SPURN HIM."

In this state of things, a petition from some of the inhabitants of the District *against* abolition was put into the hands of Mr. Clay, and he determined to make such a use of it, as might save him from being rejected and spurned by the South. Accordingly, a SPEECH in support of the petitions was prepared, *submitted to the consideration of his friends*, and finally delivered in the Senate of the United States on the 7th Feb., 1839. In this memorable *document* he vindicates the Senate from all intentional violation of the right of petition in their mode of disposing of the abolition petitions—he declares himself " irresistibly impelled to do whatever is in his power to dissuade the public from continuing to agitate a subject fraught with the most direful consequences." He distinguishes the abolitionists from those who are content to keep their conscientious objections against slavery to themselves, and from those who think the

constitutional right of petition has been invaded by
Congress ; and then draws a false and distorted picture of those whom he pleases to term " the real
ultra abolitionists." With these men, he tells us, " the
deficiency of the power of the General Government
is nothing—the acknowledged and incontestible
powers of the States are nothing—civil war, and dis-
solution of the Union, and the overthrow of a government, in which are concentrated the fondest hopes of
the civilized world, are nothing." That it may not
be supposed he *now* rejoices in " the working of
British philanthropy," he declares, " if the British
Parliament treated the West India slaves as freemen,
it also treated West India freemen as SLAVES."
Daniel O'Connell, on account of his indignant rebukes
of American Slavery, is denounced by the Kentucky
Senator, as " the plunderer of his own country, and the
libeller of a foreign and kindred people." He then
turns to the District of Columbia, and in this focus of
the American slave trade, and slave ships, and slave
prisons, and slave coffles, and slave auctions, he as-
serts that slavery, " exists here in the mildest and
most mitigated form," and he argues that Congress
cannot rightfully abolish it. On the American slave
trade, he is very explicit and logical : " I deny that
the General Government has any authority whatever
from the Constitution to abolish what is called the
slave trade, or, in other words, to prohibit the removal of slaves from one slave State to another
slave State. The grant in the Constitution" (of power
to Congress to regulate commerce between the States)
" is of a power of *regulation* and not prohibition."
Mr. Clay's perception of the distinction between

regulation and prohibition, was not so clear before he became a candidate for the Presidency. In an address he made to the Kentucky Colonization Society in 1829, after calling the *African* Slave trade " the most abominable traffic that ever disgraced the annals of the human race," he alluded to the act of Congress *prohibiting* it, and remarked, " on the 2d of March, 1807, the Act was passed, for which it was my *happy lot to vote.*" " The grant in the Constitution," under which Mr. Clay voted for the Act *prohibiting* the trade was that of power to Congress " to *regulate* foreign commerce."

As if to apologize for having in his youthful days, advocated emancipation in Kentucky, he refers in his Speech to the inconsiderable number of Slaves then in the State : " but," he adds, " if I had been then, or were NOW, a citizen of any of the planting States— the Southern or Southwestern States—I should have opposed, and would continue to oppose, any scheme whatever of emancipation, GRADUAL or IMMEDIATE." In 1797, Mr. Clay was anxious that the Kentucky Convention should take measures " for the eradication of slavery." In 1838, a law was passed submitting to the people the expediency of calling another Convention. Mr. Clay avows that, "emancipation had its influence" in procuring the passage of this law ; but in regard to the proposed Convention, by which his early wishes might have been consummated, he tells us, " *I felt myself constrained to take immediate, bold, and decided ground against it !*" Yet this is the man who, a few years since, would not exchange the satisfaction of being instrumental in eradicating slavery from his country, " for all the honor

of all the triumphs ever decreed to the most successful conqueror !" Verily, slavery has achieved a triumph, that attests its withering power over exalted
genius and high and generous aspirations—a triumph
for which humanity must weep, and patriotism
blush.

We are now prepared to investigate the direct action of the Federal Government in behalf of slavery ;
and commencing with appointments to office, we will
proceed to trace this action, first, in laws and measures
of a local and private nature, and then in attempts to
promote the general interests and perpetuity of the
institution.

APPOINTMENTS TO OFFICE.

As the citizens of the free States, are nearly double
in number to those of the slave States, it might naturally be supposed that the former would furnish the larger
share of the great officers of the Union. To such
as have indulged this supposition, the following extract from a speech lately delivered in the Senate of
the United States, by Mr. Davis of Massachusetts,
will no doubt afford very startling information.
" This interest (slavery) has ruled the destinies of
the republic. For FORTY out of FORTY EIGHT years,
it has given us a President from its own territory
and of its own selection. During all this time, it has
not only had a President, sustaining its own peculiar
views of public policy, but through him, has held and
used in its own way, the whole organization of all
the departments, and all the vast and controlling
patronage incident to that office, to aid it in carrying

on its views and policy, as well as to protect and secure to it every advantage.

"Let us explore a little further and see how the
houses of Congress have been organized. For
THIRTY years out of THIRTY SIX, that interest has
placed *its own speaker* in the chair of the other
House, thus securing the organization of committees,
and the great influence of that station. And, sir,
while all other interests have, during part of the time,
had the chair (vice presidency) in which you preside
assigned to them as *an equivalent* for these great con-
cessions, yet in each year, when a President *pro tem.*
is elected, who upon the contingencies mentioned in
the Constitution, will be the President of the United
States, that interest has INVARIABLY given us that
office. Look, I beseech you, through all the places of
honor, of profit, and privilege ; and there you will find
the representatives of this interest in numbers that
indicate its influence. Does not, then, this interest rule,
guide, and adapt public policy to its own views, and
fit it to suit the action and products of its own labor ?"

Let us see how far the *present* amount of slave interest in the Federal Government justifies the general
statement made by Mr. Davis. The presidential
chair, it is true, is filled by a northern man ; but he is
one who pledged himself to this interest before he
was elected ; who had manifested his devotion to
this interest, by giving his vote for a censorship of
the press, for the avowed purpose of restraining the
circulation of Anti-Slavery papers ; and who was
elected to his present station by southern votes !
Be it recollected, moreover, that the southern journals have insisted that a *northern* man with *southern*

4

principles, could more effectually subserve this interest as President, than a slaveholder.

In the office of Vice President, we have a slaveholder from Kentucky, presiding over the deliberations of the Senate.

A slaveholder is seated in the chair of the House of Representatives, appointing committees on the District of Columbia, enforcing gag resolutions against such as would repeal or modify the laws of Congress violating the rights of man, and deciding all questions of order in discussions bearing upon the GREAT INTEREST.

A desire is now manifested by the South to bring into the Supreme Court of the United States certain questions touching the rights and duties of the free States, relative to slaves who may come or be brought within their limits. Since the year 1830 there have been FIVE appointments to the bench of this court; and ALL from slave States. The majority of the court, including the Chief Justice, are citizens of those States. But when these questions come before the court, it may be highly important for the slaveholders to have an ATTORNEY GENERAL to argue them, in whom they can confide. Accordingly the office is filled by Mr. GRUNDY, who lately evinced his qualifications for the station, by expressing in his place as Senator from Tennessee, his approbation of LYNCH LAW, as applied to abolitionists. At the head of the department of STATE, whence issue instructions for conventions and treaties, protecting the African slave trade from British cruisers, and the American slave trade from the interference of British colonial authorities; and also for conventions for the return of fugitive slaves, is placed a gentleman from GEORGIA.

At the court of Great Britain we are represented by a slaveholder from Virginia, who, under the direction of the gentleman from Georgia, is bargaining about the value of shipwrecked negroes, and threatening the British government with the vengeance of the Republic, if it shall hereafter dare to liberate slaves who may be forced into its colonies.

At the head of the NAVY DEPARTMENT we behold a citizen of the north, enjoying the reward of his labor, in concocting one of the most virulent volumes in vindication of slavery, and vituperation of its opponents, that has ever issued from the press.

A slaveholder from SOUTH CAROLINA, distinguished for his negotiation in Mexico for the surrender of fugitive slaves, presides over the WAR DEPARTMENT.

KENTUCKY furnishes a POST MASTER GENERAL whose devotion to the " interest " had led him to authorize every Post Master to act as censor of the press, and to take from the mails every paper adverse to slavery. Thus have the slaveholders seized upon the Federal Government, and converted, as we shall presently see, what was intended as the palladium of liberty, into the shield of despotism.

THE FEDERAL GOVERNMENT AND THE TERRITORIAL LAWS OF FLORIDA.

By the Constitution, Congress have " power to dispose of and make all needful regulations respecting the territory belonging to the United States." Under this provision the territorial legislatures are permitted to enact laws which are in force till abrogated by Congress, and that body legislates directly for the territories whenever it thinks proper. Hence it is morally responsible for the territorial legislation.

On the 11th February, 1834, Messrs. J. & M. Garnett and *Maria* Garnett, all of Virginia, presented a petition to Congress, setting forth that they were the owners of certain slaves whom they hired to persons in Florida ; and that by a law of the territory a tax of ten dollars was imposed on every slave owned by a non-resident ; and they prayed Congress to relieve them from the payment of this tax. It was obvious that this tax tended to discourage slaveholders from sending their slaves into Florida and there hiring them at high rates to the new settlers, who had not capital enough immediately to stock their plantations. Congress, without hesitation, abolished the tax. The law thus annulled, was not in itself revolting to justice or humanity. But there was *then*, and still is, a law of Florida of a very different character.

On the 4th February, 1832, it was enacted that whenever a judgment for debt was recovered in the territory against a free negro or mulatto, and the judgment was not satisfied in *five* days, *the debtor should be* SOLD *at auction to pay the judgment.* Imprisonment for debt is now deemed a relic of barbarism, but here we have an instance of insolvent debtors being SOLD for the benefit of their creditors, virtually by the authority, and directly with the sanction of the Congress of the United States!! The practical operation of this law is to convert free negroes into slaves. A recent sale under it will illustrate its character. Within a few months a free negro was sold at Appalachicola for TEN years, to satisfy a debt which, *including legal costs*, amounted to seventy dollars ; so that his services were valued at seven dollars a year! The common wages paid in that part of the country

for slave labor, may be learned from the following notice, taken from the Brunswick (Ga.) Advertiser, 25th January, 1838. " *Wanted to hire*.—The undersigned wish to hire one thousand negroes, to work on the Brunswick canal, of whom one-third may be women. Sixteen dollars per month will be paid for steady, prime men, and thirteen dollars for able *women*. F. & A. PRATT.
P. M. NIGHTENGALE."

It is obvious that a sale under this law, for a *term of years*, is equivalent to a sale for life. The debtor may be sold from hand to hand, and at the expiration of his term may find himself under the lash of a driver in Louisiana or Missouri, without the possibility of proving his title to freedom. Yet, a proposition in Congress to repeal this most inhuman and profligate law would be laid upon the table, and not a representative of the people be permitted to say a word on the subject.

ACTION OF CONGRESS IN BEHALF OF THE SLAVEHOLDERS OF LOUISIANA.

On the 31st of May, 1830, the House of Representatives adopted a resolution, directing the Secretary of the Treasury to ascertain and report the number of hands (slaves) required per acre in the sugar cultivation. The Secretary accordingly issued a circular, proposing a number of interrogatories respecting the cultivation of sugar, and among others, the following : " The number of hands (slaves) required to cultivate a given quantity of land planted with cane, and to perform all the labor necessary in the manu-
4*

facture of sugar in the different places where it is made ?"

This circular was widely distributed, and the answers returned to it were published at public expense ; and thus were the sugar growers instructed, by means of the Federal Government, with what number of slaves to stock their plantations ; what ex-- pense they must incur in feeding and clothing them, and what number of *new* slaves they must annually procure to keep up the " force." From the information thus furnished, it appeared that the destruction of slaves in this culture is so great, that there is a yearly excess of deaths over births of TWO AND A HALF PER CENT.* This waste of life is supplied from the breeding farms of Maryland and Virginia. Turning from this private and local action of the Federal Government, we will now take a view of its enlarged and comprehensive efforts for the general protection and perpetuity of the slave system. The advocates of that system have always looked with distrust and alarm upon the free colored people, and have deemed it good policy to prevent their acquisition of power and influence : hence the

EFFORTS OF THE FEDERAL GOVERNMENT TO OPPRESS
AND DEGRADE THE FREE PEOPLE OF COLOR.

The Constitution of the United States acknowledges no right or disqualification founded on complexion ; but those who have administered it, have made the tincture of the *skin* of far greater importance than the qualities of either the head or the

* See Report of Secretary of the Treasury, January 19, 1831.

heart.   So early as 1790, Congress passed an act prescribing the mode in which " any alien, being a WHITE
person," might be naturalized and admitted to the
rights of an American citizen.

Two years after, an act was passed for organizing
the militia, which was to consist of " each and every
free, able-bodied WHITE male citizen," &c.   No other
government on earth prohibits any portion of its citizens from participating in the national defence ; and
this strange and degrading prohibition, utterly repugnant to the principles both of the Declaration of Independence and of the Constitution, marks the solicitude of the Federal Government to pursue the policy
most agreeable to the slaveholders.   But not content
with this insult to colored citizens, another, and
perhaps a still more wanton and malignant one,
was offered by the Government in the act of 1810,
organizing the Post Office Department.   The 4th
Section enacts that " no other than a free WHITE
person shall be employed in carrying the mail of
the United States, either as post-rider or *driver* of
a carriage carrying the mail," under a penalty of
fifty dollars.

Any vagabond from Europe, any fugitive from our
own prisons, may take charge of the United States
mail ; but a native born American citizens, of unim-
peachable morals, and with property acquired by honest industry, may not, if his *skin* be dark, guide the
horses which draw the carriage in which a bag of
newspapers is deposited !*

* The following letter of instruction from the Postmaster General to one of his deputies, written in 1828, is a curious commentary
on this law.

Such are the insults heaped by the Federal Government on the colored citizens throughout the States: let us see what conduct it pursues towards them *on its own territory*, over which it possesses " exclusive jurisdiction."

In 1820, Congress passed a law authorizing the WHITE citizens of the city of Washington to elect WHITE city officers; thus making a *white skin* an indispensable qualification for both suffrage and office. The officers thus elected were specially empowered by the national legislature "to prescribe the terms and conditions on which *free negroes and mulattoes* may reside in the city." In pursuance of this grant of power, the *white* officers passed an ordinance (May 31, 1827) requiring all the free colored persons then in Washington and wishing to remain, to be registered; and enacting, that if any free man with a colored skin should presume to *play at cards*, or even to be *present* while *another* free colored person was playing, he should be fined not exceeding five dollars; that if he should have a *dance* in his house, without permission from the *white* Mayor, he should be fined not exceeding ten dollars; that should he take the liberty to go out of his own house *after ten o'clock at night*, without a pass from a Justice of the Peace, or

" SIR,—The mail may not, in any case whatever, be in the custody of a *colored* person. If a colored person is employed to lift the mail from the stage into the post office, it does not pass into his custody, but the labor is performed in the presence and under the immediate direction of the WHITE person who has it in custody : but if a *colored* person takes it from a tavern and carries it himself to the post-office, it comes into his custody during the time of carrying it; which is contrary to law.   I am, &c.,

JOHN McLEAN.

" some respectable citizen," (!) he might be compelled
to pass the rest of the night " in a lock-up house,"
and the next morning be fined ten dollars ; and should
any dark complexioned free man be guilty of drunk-
enness or profane language, he should be fined not
exceeding three dollars. Thus we see with what zeal
the Washington Corporation endeavors to prevent
the colored citizens from affecting the manners and
fashions of their white brethren. But there are still
more serious matters. A colored citizen from any
of the States, taking up his residence in the Capital
of the Republic, is required within a certain time, not
only to be registered, but also to find *two freehold
sureties* in the penalty of five hundred dollars, for his
good behavior ; and if he does not, he is to be imprisoned till he consents to leave the seat of the
Federal Government ; and if he does not *prove* that
he is a freeman, he shall be *sold as a slave to pay his
jail fees !!*

In 1830, a bill to establish the territorial government of Iowa was before Congress. A slaveholder
from Alabama moved to exclude colored persons
from the right of suffrage ; and the obedient Senate
consented.*

Such are the abominable and iniquitous means used
by and with the sanction of Congress for the degradation and oppression of colored citizens. We are
next to take a view of

* In 1787, when our fathers established the government of the
Northwestern Territory, they prohibited slavery, and disfranchised
no man on account of his complexion.

SLAVERY UNDER THE AUTHORITY OF THE FEDERAL GOVERNMENT.

It is well known that Congress is the local legislature of the District of Columbia, and of all the territories belonging to the Union, and with powers far exceeding those possessed by any State Legislature, being unfettered with constitutional restrictions. The authority vested in Congress over the District and territories, is virtually despotic, being "an exclusive jurisdiction in all cases whatsoever." Yet we have long had slaveholding territories. The vast domain acquired by the purchase of Louisiana, has, under the authority of Congress, been stocked with slaves, excepting so much as is north of 36½° north latitude, which is, by Act of Congress, specially protected from the pollution. This very law is one of the most decided acts of the Federal Government in behalf of slavery; for by means of it, the immense territory south of this line was deliberately surrendered to all the cruelties and abominations of the system; it was moreover an express acknowledgment by the Government of its power to prohibit slavery throughout the *whole* territory, and that it had made a COMPROMISE, a bargain between humanity and cruelty, religion and wickedness; and had erected, on an arbitrary line, a partition wall between slavery and liberty.

But it is in the District of Columbia, and under the shadow of the proud Capitol, that the action of the Federal Government in behalf of slavery is exhibited in its most odious and disgusting forms. We shall have occasion presently to exhibit the seat of the National Government, as the great slave mart of the

North American continent, "furnished with all appliances and means to boot." The old slave laws of Virginia and Maryland, marked by the barbarity of other days, form by Act of Congress the slave code of the District. Of this code, a single sample will suffice. A slave convicted of setting fire to a building, shall have his head cut off, and his body divided into quarters, and the parts set up in the most public places! But let it not be supposed that Congress has not itself legislated directly on the subject of slavery. An Act of 15th May, 1820, gives the Corporation of Washington power to "punish corporeally any SLAVE for a breach of any of their ordinances." Happy would it have been for the honor of our country, if the sympathies of its rulers in behalf of slavery, had been exhibited only on the national domain ; but they pervade every portion of the confederacy, as is but too apparent in

THE INTERFERENCE OF THE FEDERAL GOVERNMENT FOR THE RECOVERY OF FUGITIVE SLAVES.

The Federal Constitution contains the following clause : "No person held to service or labor in one State under the laws thereof, escaping into another, shall in consequence of any law or regulation therein be discharged from such service or labor, but shall be delivered up on claim of the party to whom such service or labor may be due."

At the time this constitution was adopted, the cultivation and manufacture of cotton had not so far progressed, as to paralyze, by their profits, the conscience of the nation, or to divest it of the sense of

shame; and hence this clause, although relating to
slaves, forbears to name them. It was inserted to
satisfy the South; and its obvious meaning is, that
slaves escaping into States in which slavery is abolished by law, shall not *therefore* be deemed free by
the State authorities, but shall be delivered by those
authorities to his master. This clause imposes an
obligation on the States, but confers no power on
Congress; and the Constitution moreover declares,
that "the powers not delegated to the United States
by the Constitution, nor prohibited by it to the States,
are reserved to the States respectively, or to the people." Hence it follows, that as the power of recover-
ing these fugitives is not delegated to Congress, it is
reserved to the several States, who are bound to make
such laws as may be deemed proper, to authorize the
master to recover his slave. Nevertheless, the Federal Government in its zeal for slavery, has not scru-
pled to assume power never delegated to it, and has
exercised that power in contemptuous violation of
every principle, which in free countries directs the
administration of justice. If a Virginian enters New-
York, and claims as his property a horse which he
finds in the possession of one of our citizens, an impartial jury is selected to pass on his claim,—witnesses are orally and publicly examined,—the claimant is debarred from all private intercourse with the
jury; and when the trial is over, the jury retire to
deliberate on their verdict, under the charge of an
officer, who is sworn to keep them apart, and not to
suffer any person to speak with them; nor can the horse
be at last recovered but with the unanimous consent
of the jury. But let the Virginian claim, not the

horse, but the CITIZEN HIMSELF, as his beast of burden, and the Federal Government makes all things easy for him. By the Act of 1793, the slaveholder may himself, without oath, or process of any kind, seize his prey, where he can find him, and at his leisure, (for no time is specified,) drag him before any Justice of the Peace in the place, whom he may prefer.* This justice is a state officer, and of the lowest judicial grade, and under no legal obligation to execute an Act of Congress, and entitled to no fees for his services. He is therefore peculiarly accessible to improper influences. Before this magistrate, who is not authorized to compel the attendance of witnesses in such a case, the slaveholder brings his victim, and if he can satisfy this judge of his own choice, "by oral testimony or *affidavit*," and for aught that appears in the law, by his own oath, that his claim is well founded, the wretched prisoner is surrendered to him as a slave for life, torn from his wife and children, bereft of all the rights of humanity, and converted into a chattel,—an article of merchandise,—a beast of burden ! !

The Federal Constitution declares:—"In suits at common law, where the value in controversy shall exceed *twenty dollars*, the right of TRIAL BY JURY shall be preserved ; but the Act of 1793, in suits in which "the value in controversy" exceeds all estimation,

* In New-York the legislature has interfered, and forbidden a Justice of the Peace to act, and has therefore virtually declared the Act of Congress to be unconstitutional,—and that the power of prescribing the mode in which fugitives shall be restored, belongs exclusively to the States.

dispenses with trial by jury, and indeed with almost every safeguard of justice and personal liberty.

This law, iniquitous as it is, does not require State officers to *anticipate* the pursuit of the slaveholder, and to seize and imprison their fellow-men, on mere suspicion that they *may* be claimed as slaves. What the Federal Government dares not do in the States, it accomplishes on its own exclusive territory, and in a manner which, for atrocious wickedness and tyranny, leaves far in the shade, the vilest acts of European despotism. This is indeed strong language ; but alas ! language is too feeble adequately to represent the turpitude of the laws and practices sanctioned by the Federal Government, in the District under its " exclusive jurisdiction.

By the Act of -1793, a justice can take no step for the restoration of a fugitive slave, till the fact of his being one is proved before him on oath. But in the Metropolis of the Nation,—in the city called by the name of the Father of his Country, a Justice of the Peace may commit to the UNITED STATES PRISON, and and into the custody of the UNITED STATES MARSHAL, any man he may choose to suspect of being a fugitive slave. Notice is then given in the newspapers of the commitment, and the unknown owner is warned to take away his property, or it will be sold according to LAW, to pay JAIL FEES.

After the doors of the dungeon have closed upon the victim, no magistrate, no court, no jury take cognizance of his claims of freedom. The jailor is the only tribunal to which he can appeal, and how *disinterested* a tribunal will presently be seen. If a freeman, no master can of course lawfully claim him, and not being claimed, he is sold at auction to raise money to pay an officer of the Federal Government for the trouble and expense of keeping him a few weeks in prison. What civilized government of the old world practices more execrable wickedness ?*

The whole depth of this villany is not yet sounded. The disclosures we are now about making should make every ear to tingle and every heart to quake. No doubt it will occur to many that if a free man, all the prisoner has to do, to obtain his liberation, is to prove his freedom.—Prove his freedom while locked up in his cell! Where is his counsel ?—where his process for commanding the attendance of witnesses ? where the court sitting in open day to investigate his right to freedom ? where the jury to pass upon his case ? The marshal, or his deputy the jailor, is the only human being, except his fellow-victims, to whom he can tell his tale. The marshal is the judge, and the sole judge of his prisoner's title to freedom. He is the arbiter of happiness and misery, of liberty and bondage : he opens the door of the dungeon, and at his sovereign will bids his captive go forth to enjoy the rights and fulfil the duties of a rational, account-

* Not as an apology for this expression, but as a reason why the writer feels more sensibly than perhaps many others on this subject, he thinks proper to mention that a free colored man belonging to his neighborhood in West Chester County, N. Y., on going to Washington some years since, was there legally kidnapped, and and advertised by the Marshal to be sold to pay his jail fees. A Washington paper containing the advertisement providentially fell into the hands of a citizen of the County who knew the man. A public meeting was called, and the Govenor of the State, De Witt Clinton, at their request, demanded from the President his immediate release as a citizen of New York.

able, and immortal being, or conducts him to the
human shambles erected in the city of Washington,
and there sells him under the hammer as a SLAVE FOR
LIFE. Compared with this tremendous jurisdiction,
the powers vested in the highest judicial officer in
our country dwindle into insignificance. And should
such a judge be disinterested ? The very question is
shocking to our every idea of justice. Disinterested!
Screened from the public eye—accountable only to
that Being who seeth in secret—declaring his judgment in the recesses of the prison, he should of all
men be most exempt from human passion and in-
firmity. *Yet to this judge the law offers a high and
tempting bribe to sell men he knows to be free, and thus to
become a manufacturer of slaves.* Will this statement
be credited ? It cannot, and ought not to be, without full and unequivocal proof, and to that proof we
now appeal ; premising for the better understanding
of our proof, that the marshal is required to maintain
the suspected fugitives while in his custody and is
entitled to fees for receiving them, &c., and if un-
reclaimed, has no means of procuring payment of his
expenses and fees but from the proceeds of the sale
of his prisoners ; and further, that the *whole* of those
proceeds are permitted by law to remain in his
pocket, unless *after* the sale the master should be
discovered, and should claim the balance.

On the 11th January, 1827, the committee on the
District of Columbia, to whom the subject had been
referred by the House of Representatives, reported
that " in this District, as in all the slaveholding
States in the Union, the legal presumption is, that
persons of color going at large without any eviden-

ces of their freedom, are absconding slaves, and
primâ facie liable to all the legal provisions applicable to that class of persons." They state that in the
part of the District ceded by Virginia, a FREE negro
may be arrested and put in jail for three months on
suspicion of being a fugitive ; he is then to be hired
out to pay his *jail fees ;* and if he does not prove his
freedom within twelve months, is to be sold as a
SLAVE. This statement is followed by the remark,
" the committee do not consider any alteration of the
law in the County of Alexandria in relation to this
subject, necessary !" In the County of Washington,
ceded by Maryland, they inform us, " If a *free* man
of color should be apprehended as a runaway, he is
subjected to the payment of all *fees and rewards* given
by law for apprehending runaways ; and upon failure
to make such payment, is liable to be sold as a slave."
That is, a man *acknowledged to be free,* and unaccused of
any offence, is to be sold as a *slave* to pay the " fees
and rewards given by law for apprehending *runaways.*"
If Turkish despotism is disgraced by any enactment of
equal atrocity, we are ignorant of the fact. Even the
committee thought this law rather hard, and therefore they " recommended such an alteration of it as
would make such charges payable by the corporation
of Washington.* But the Federal Government, un-
wavering in its devotion to slavery, made no alteration, and the code of Washington is to this day polluted by unquestionably the most iniquitous statute
in Christendom. Laws are sometimes more profligate
than those who are called to administer them, and
the committee assure us that the Marshal has in all

---

* See Reports of Committee, 2 Sess. 19 Cong. Vol. I. No. 43.

cases refrained from selling his prisoners for fees and charges, when their right to freedom has been established ; and in consequence of not availing himself of the privilege allowed him by this law, he had incurred, in the last eight years, a personal loss of $500 ! In other words, the Marshal's sense of justice, decency, and humanity, exceeded that of the rulers of our Republic.

On the 29th January, 1829, the committee on the District of Columbia made a report in obedience to the instructions of the House of Representatives, " to inquire into the slave trade as it exists in and is carried on through the District." The report proposes no interference on the part of Congress, but is virtually an apology for this vile traffic, as is apparent from the following heartless sentiments and false assertions.

" The trade alluded to, is presumed to refer more particularly to that which is carried on with the view of transporting slaves to the South, which is one way of gradually diminishing the evil complained of here ; while the situation of these persons is considerably *mitigated by being transplanted to a more genial and bountiful clime.* Although violence may sometimes be done to their feelings in the separation of families, it is by the laws of society which operate upon them as property, and cannot be avoided as long as they exist ; yet it should be some consolation to those whose feelings are interested in their behalf, to know that *their condition is more frequently bettered, and their minds happier by the exchange.*"*

To this report is appended a letter (January 13, 1829,) from the Marshal to the committee, containing most important and heart-rending statements.

* Reports of Committees, 2 Sess. 20 Cong. No. 60.

It appears from this letter, that from the 1st January, 1826, to 1st January, 1828, there were committed to the Washington prison as runaways, 101.

Proved to be free, and discharged,	15
Unclaimed, and sold for maintenance, and charges, and fees,	5
Proved to be slaves, and delivered to their masters,	81
	101

In 1828—Committed as runaways, 78.

Proved to be free,	11
Unclaimed, or sold for jail fees, ect.	1
Delivered to their masters,	66
	78

Here then is proof, official documentary proof, that in three years, 179 human beings were, by the authority of the Federal Government, arrested in *one* county of the District, and committed to prison on no allegation of crime, but merely to aid the slaveholders in trampling upon those great principles of human rights, for the protection of which the National Government was professedly founded. It is also in proof, that of these 179 prisoners, 26 were, by the confession of the Marshal, *free* men ; men whom (as appears from the report we have quoted,) he had a *legal* right to consign to hopeless and awful bondage, merely because they were too poor to pay the expenses of their unjust imprisonment ; and who were indebted for their liberty, not to the laws and constitution of their country, but to the beneficence of their jailor—a beneficence too, exercised at his own pecuniary loss. Proof also is here given, that six persons unclaimed as slaves, were, by the judgment of this same jailor, without counsel, witnesses, or trial, sentenced to be sold as slaves for the purpose of raising money, the whole of which, as we shall presently see, was paid over to the Judge who pronounced the sentence. The Marshal gives in his letter the particulars of the sale of five unclaimed negroes, as follows, viz.

Si—Amount of jail fees, etc.	$84 82

Offered for sale according to law and no person being willing to give $84 82, he was purchased by Tench Ringgold, the Marshal, for that sum, and afterwards sold by him to Robert Bown for $20, by which the Marshal lost, 64 82

Hannah Green sold for	$61 00
Maintenance, &c.	48 71
Balance remaining in Marshal's hands,	$12 29
Lewis Davis sold for	$250 00
Amount of fees, &c.	50 07
Balance remaining in Marshal's hands,	$199 93
James Green sold for	$80 00
Fees and maintenance,	49 66
Balance remaining in Marshal's hands,	$30 34
Arthur Neal sold for amount of his jail fees and maintenance, to the Marshal, being	$46 06
Sold afterwards by private sale to J. G. Hutton for	40 00
Lost by Marshal,	$06 06

The letter concludes thus : " The Marshal has always considered it to be his duty, whenever a negro was committed as a runaway by a Justice of the Peace, who in all cases under the law commits them, which negro had not in his possession proof of his freedom, but alleged himself to be a freeman, to write to any part of the United States to persons who the negro affirmed could prove his freedom, urging them to send on their certificates of such negro being free; and in many instances, these letters of the Marshal or his jailor have been the means of bringing proof that the negro was free.

" The law of Maryland in force in this District, directs that the balance of sales of negroes (sold as runaways) *shall remain in the Marshal's hands* until the runaway was identified as the property of some master; and in conformity thereto, the Marshal has uniformly handed over such balance whenever the master proved his property. In a late case, Mr. Sprigg, of Louisiana, lost a valuable slave, who escaped from him, and made his way to this District, and was committed to my custody, advertised and sold, according to law; leaving a balance of *five hundred dollars*, after paying maintenance, &c., in my hand. The negro was carried to Louisiana by the person who purchased him of me, discovered by his former master, Mr. Sprigg, who sent on here and claimed his money. Having ascertained that this negro was the property of Mr. Sprigg, I paid the $500 on demand to his agent here, Mr. Josiah Johnson, Senator of Congress from that State.

TENCH RINGGOLD, Marshal Dist. Col."

Such are the secrets of the prison-house, established

by the Federal Government. It may be well to con-
template them in detail. It appears from the cases of
SI and NEAL, that the Marshal of the United States,
after deciding on the liberty or bondage of his prisoners, is allowed to take his *fees* in human flesh, and the
condemned becomes the *property* of the very judge
who sentenced him to servitude, and who carries him
into the market there to make out of him as much
money as he can. True it is, Mr. Ringgold's specula-
tions appear not to have been very productive, but
other jailor-judges may have less honesty, or more
skill in negro flesh. The Marshal, it seems, sold his
fees in the shape of SI, for only $20. No reason is
assigned for this nominal price. Very probably it
was a case similar to the one described by Mr. Miner,
in his speech on the floor of the House of Representatives, in 1829. "In August, 1821," said Mr. M.,
"a black man was taken up, and imprisoned as a runaway. He was kept confined until October, 1822,
four hundred and five days. In this time, vermin,
disease, and misery had deprived him of the use of
his limbs. He was rendered a cripple for life, and
finally discharged, *as no one would buy him.*"

The Hannah and James Green sold for fees, were
most likely man and wife, and may remind us that the
law we are considering is utterly reckless of the most
sacred relations. The proceeds of three of the five
sold in 1826–7, after deducting fees, &c., is $242 56;
and this sum, according to law, the Marshal retains
till called for ; but if the negroes were free, then, there
being no claimant, the money can never be called
for, and becomes the perquisite of office ; and the income of the Judge of course fluctuates according to

the number of freemen he condemns to slavery. Thus does the law literally press upon the Marshal the wages of unrighteousness—thus does it bribe him to the commission of wickedness. In one instance, the receipts of a single condemnation were $500, of which the Marshal was deprived only by a most extraordinary accident.

And now let us review the conduct of the Federal Government towards the free colored citizen of any State, who presumes to visit the city of Washington. At the will of a Justice of the Peace he is thrown into prison. His jailor, if he possesses the humanity and disinterestedness of Mr. Ringgold, may, if he pleases, write letters to distant parts of the confederacy, although he knows that a favorable answer may keep some hundred dollars from finding their way into his pocket. If no such answer arrives, without any evidence that the letter of inquiry was ever received, the poor wretch is condemned as a slave, and the price of his bones and muscles is paid to the judge who condemned him.

And by whom is this accursed law kept in force? By *northern* Representatives and Senators in Congress. On the 8th February, 1836, the House of Representatives resolved, that "Congress ought not to interfere in *any way* with slavery in the District of Columbia," and no less than 82 northern men had the hardihood to record their names in favor of the resolution. To place, if possible, in a still stronger light, the conduct of these men, it may be mentioned that the law we have been considering, belonged to the code of Maryland, at the time the District was ceded, and was continued in force by Act of Congress. In the mean-

time, the Legislature of Maryland, composed of slaveholders, yielding to the spirit of the age, has erased
this foul stain from her statute-book, while our
northern democrats, with liberty and equality for-
ever on their lips, in hope of getting a few southern votes for their party, discover that Congress
ought not to interfere in any way with slavery in
the District, although it is by the authority of Congress that freemen are there converted into slaves.

We will now place side by side, two advertisements, one published by authority of Congress, in
which northern men have the majority; the other
by authority of the slave State of Maryland,—the
first relating to a *woman* and *infant* claiming to be
FREE, the other to a man confessing himself a SLAVE.

"NOTICE.—Was committed to the jail of Washington county, District of Columbia, as a runaway,
a negro WOMAN, by the name of Polly Leiper, and
her *infant* child William. * * * * Says she
was set free by John Campbell, of Richmond, Va.
in 1818 or 1819. The owner of the above-described
woman and *child*, if any, are requested to come and
prove them, and take them away, or *they* will be
SOLD FOR THEIR JAIL FEES AND OTHER EXPENSES AS THE
LAW DIRECTS.   TENCH RINGGOLD,
    May 19, 1827.   *Marshal.*"

"RANAWAY.—Was committed to the jail of Washington County, Maryland, on the 24th December
last, a mulatto man who calls himself *John Mc-
Daniel*, about 25 years of age. * * Says he be-
longs to William Hill, living at Falmouth, Va., and
was sold to John Daily, living somewhere in the

South. The owner of the said slave is requested to come and take him away, or *he will be released*, *according to law.* CHRISTIAN NEWCOMB, Jun., DECEMBER 10, 1827.* *Sheriff.*"

The endeavors of the Federal Government to secure the restoration of fugitive slaves to their masters, are not confined either to the District of Columbia, or to the States of this confederacy. Even American diplomacy must be made subservient to the interests of the slaveholders, and republican ambassadors must bear to foreign courts the wailings of our government for the escape of human property.

On the 10th of May, 1828, the House of Representatives requested the President "to open a negotiation with the British Government, in the view to obtain an arrangement whereby fugitive slaves who have taken refuge in the Canadian provinces of that government, may be surrendered by the functionaries thereof to their masters, upon making satisfactory proof of their ownership of said slaves."

Here was a plain, palpable interference in behalf of slavery by a government which we are often assured by the slaveholders, "has nothing to do with slavery ;" and so tame and subservient were the northern members, that this disgraceful resolution was adopted without even a division of the House ! At the next session, the impatience of the slaveholders to know if Great Britain would restore their slaves who had taken refuge in Canada, could brook

* Both advertisements are taken from the Washington Intelligencer.

6

no longer delay, and the House called on the President to inform them of the result of the negotiation. The President immediately submitted a mass of documents to the House, from which it appeared that the zeal of the Executive, in behalf of "the peculiar institution," had *anticipated* the wishes of the Legislature. Two years *before* the interference of the House, viz., on the 19th of June, 1826, Mr. Clay, Secretary of State, had instructed Mr. Gallatin, American Minister in London, to propose a stipulation for "a mutual surrender of all persons held to service or labor under the laws of either party who escape into the territories of the other." Mr. Clay dwelt on the number of fugitives in Canada, and desired Mr. Gallatin to press on the British Government the consideration that such a stipulation would secure *to the West India planters the recovery of such of their slaves as might take refuge in the American Republic !*

Surely the Federal Government was never intended by its founders to act the part of kidnapper for West India slaveholders.

On the 24th of February, 1827, Mr. Clay again urged Mr. Gallatin to procure this stipulation, and informed him that a treaty had just been concluded with Mexico, *by which that power had engaged to restore our runaway slaves.*

On the 5th of July, 1827, Mr. Gallatin communicated to his government the answer of the British Minister, that "it was utterly impossible for them

* Such a treaty was negotiated, but the Mexican Congress refused to ratify the base compact.

to agree to a stipulation for the surrender of fugitive slaves."

Determined not to take NO for an answer, Mr. Clay desired Mr. Barbour, our then Minister in England, to renew the negotiation, inasmuch as the escape of slaves into Canada is " a growing evil;" but alas! Mr. Barbour replied, that on broaching the subject to the British Minister, he had informed him "*the law of Parliament gave freedom to every slave who effected his landing on British ground.*"* To have attempted to march an army into Canada, for the purpose of seizing these fugitives, would have cost rather more than they were worth. There was, however, a territory on our southern frontier, belonging to a power less able than Great Britain to punish aggressions on her sovereignty, and hence it is that we are called to consider

THE INVASION OF FLORIDA, AND DESTRUCTION OF FUGITIVE SLAVES BY THE FORCES OF THE FEDERAL GOVERNMENT.

On the 15th March, 1816, Mr. Crawford, Secretary of War, addressed a letter to General Jackson, informing him that there was a fort in Florida, occupied by between two hundred and fifty and three hundred blacks, and that they and the hostile Creek Indians were guilty of secret practices to inveigle negroes from the frontiers of Georgia, and directing him to call the attention of the Commandant at Pensacola to the subject. The Secretary added, that should the Commandant decline interfering, and

* State papers, 2 Sess. 20th Congress, Vol. I.

should it be determined that the destruction of the negro fort does not require the sanction of Congress, me-ns will be promptly taken for its reduction.

General Jackson, however had, *before* the receipt of this despatch, "assumed the responsibility" of sending his orders respecting this very fort to Gen. Gaines. "If the fort harbors the negroes of our citizens, or of friendly Indians living within our territory, or holds out inducements to the slaves of our citizens to desert from their owner's service, *it must be destroyed.* Notify the governor of Pensacola of your *advance into his territory, and for the express purpose of destroying these lawless banditti.*" The letter concludes with directions to "restore the stolen negroes to their rightful owners." (Letter of 8th April, 1816.)

Owing to some cause not explained, Gen. Gaines did not fulfil his instructions; and a gun boat was sent up the Appalachicola river by order of Commodore Patterson, and on the 27th of July attacked the fort by firing red-hot shot at it. A shot entered the magazine which exploded. The result is thus stated in the official report: "Three hundred negroes, *men, women, and children,* and about twenty Indians, were in the fort; of these, two hundred and seventy were killed, and the greater part of the rest *mortally* wounded."

Commodore Patterson, in his letter to the Secretary of the Navy, observes: "The service rendered by the destruction of this fort, and the band of negroes who held it and the country in its vicinity, is of great and manifest importance to the United States, and particularly those States bordering on the Creek nation, as it had become a general rendezvous for *runaway slaves* and disaffected Indians—an asylum where they found arms and ammunition to protect themselves against their owners and the government. This hold being destroyed, they have no longer a place to fly to, and will not be so liable to *abscond.* The force of the negroes was daily increasing, and they had commenced several plantations on the banks of the Appalachicola."*

We are not aware that this gallant achievement called forth at the time any testimony of approbation from the government. It was probably regarded as an unnecessary destruction of property. Gen. Jackson's orders were to *restore* the negroes "to their rightful owners," not to kill them. But times have changed ; abolition doctrines are spreading, and hereafter our officers, and soldiers, and sailors, may feel some reluctance at being sent on kidnapping expeditions. Hence, after the lapse of twenty-three years, the government has deemed it good policy to evince their estimation of such services, by rewarding the heroes of Appalachicola. The following is taken from the Washington Globe.

"NOTICE.—The sum of FIVE THOUSAND FOUR HUNDRED AND SIXTY-FIVE DOLLARS having been appropriated by an Act of Congress, passed at the *last* session, to be distributed as prize money among the officers and crews, their, or either of their heirs or legal representatives, of the gun boats, numbered 149 and 154 ; who in the month of July, 1816, blew up and destroyed a fort occupied by fugitive negroes and In-

* State papers. 2 Sess. 15th Cong. No. 65.
6*

dians, on the river Appalachicola, all persons having claims upon the sum so appropriated, are notified to present and prove the same without delay at the office of the Fourth Auditor of the Treasury Department, in the City of Washington.

"*Fourth Auditor's Office, May 23d, 1839.*"

It is now time to advert to one of the most extraordinary exploits of American diplomacy, viz :

COMPENSATION FOR FUGITIVE SLAVES OBTAINED BY THE FEDERAL GOVERNMENT.

The presence of British armed vessels in our southern waters, during the last war, afforded an opportunity to many of the slaves to escape from bondage. In 1814, and while the war was raging in all its fury, commissioners were appointed to treat of peace, and instructions were given to them as to the stipulations to be inserted in the treaty. These instructions contain the following remarkable passage. " The negroes taken from the southern States should be returned to their owners, or *paid* for at their full value. If these slaves were considered as non-combatants, they ought to be restored : if as property, they ought to be paid for." Moreover, this stipulation is expressly included " in the conditions on which you are to *insist* in the proposed negotiations."—*Letter of Instructions from Mr. Monroe, Secretary of State, 28th January, 1814.**

Thus we see that not even the calamities of war could divert the attention of the Federal Government from the peculiar interests of the slaveholders. The

* American State papers. Vol. IX. p. 364.

commissioners were faithful to the charge thus given to them : and in the treaty concluded at Ghent, adroitly provided for the restoration of *slaves ;* and in such obscure terms as ultimately secured a far more extensive concession than the British negotiators had any intention of making.

The 1st article is as follows : " All territory, places and possessions whatever, taken from either party, by the other during the war, or which may be taken after the signing of this treaty, shall be restored without delay ; and without causing any destruction or carrying away of the artillery or other public property *originally captured* in said forts or places, and which shall *remain* upon the exchange of the ratifications of this treaty, or any *slaves* or other private property."

The treaty was ratified at Washington on the 17th February ; and *six* days after, three commissioners appointed by the government appeared in the Chesapeake, authorized to demand and receive the slaves on board the British squadron still in our waters.

Captain John Clarelle happened to be at the moment in command of the British forces, and he positively refused to give up a single fugitive ; contending that the stipulation in the treaty related only to slaves " originally *captured* in forts or places," and remaining in such forts or places at the exchange of the ratifications, and had no reference to slaves who had voluntarily sought protection on board British vessels.

A few days after, Admiral Cockburn arrived and a similar demand was made upon him. He also refused to surrender any *fugitives,* as such were not intended in the treaty, but gave up eighty slaves which were found on Cumberland Island at the time that place was *captured*, and who had not been removed previous to the exchange of ratifications; this being a case directly within the true meaning and intention of the treaty. The Secretary of State then applied to the British Charge d' Affaires at Washington, requesting him to direct the Naval Commanders in the Chesapeake to give up the fugitives on board their vessels; but Mr. Baker declining interfering, taking the same view of the article as the Admiral had done. In the meantime, the squadron had sailed for Bermuda. The Government, tracking the scent of a fugitive with blood-hound keenness, forthwith despatched an agent to Bermuda in pursuit, to demand the negroes of the Governor. The worthy Englishman, nettled at a requisition so derogatory to the honor of his country, replied, " he would rather Bermuda, with every man, woman and child in it, were sunk under the sea, than surrender one slave that had sought protection under the flag of England."

The Agent, (Thomas Spalding,) nothing daunted, now assumed the diplomatist, and addressed a long argumentative despatch to Admiral Griffith, commanding on the Bermuda station, demanding the fugitives, and promising to furnish him with a particular list of the slaves claimed, which he expected to receive in a few days from the United States. The Admiral very cavalierly assured Mr. Spalding that it was quite unnecessary for him to wait at Bermuda for the expected document, since there was, neither at Bermuda nor any other British island or settlement, any authority " competent to deliver up persons who during the late wars, had placed themselves under the protection of the British flag."*

From British Governors and Admirals, our Government now turned to the British Cabinet, and found that there also it was held a point of honor to keep faith, even with runaway slaves. Lord Castlereagh declared that the Government never would have assented to a treaty requiring the surrender of persons who had taken refuge under the British Standard. Again was the demand made, and again was it unequivocally rejected. But the administration refused to yield, and insisted on a reference of the question to the decision of a friendly power, and named the Emperor of Russia as umpire. After tedious negotiation, this point was carried; and in 1818, a convention was concluded at London, submitting the true construction of the treaty to the Emperor, who decided in favor of the slaveholders. It now became necessary to determine how the number of slaves, and their value, should be ascertained. Another negotiation ensued, which resulted in a second convention, by which it was agreed that each party should appoint a certain number of Commissioners, who should form a Board to sit at Washington, to receive and liquidate the claims of the masters. But difficulties soon arose. The American Commissioners insisted on *interest*, which the others refused to allow. Negotiations again commenced, till at last the British Cabinet, wearied with the pertinacity of the American Government, and sick of the controversy, entered into a third convention, (13th Nov. 1826) by which the enormous sum of ONE MILLION

* State papers—14th Cong. 2d Sess.—Senate documents, No. 28.

TWO HUNDRED AND FOUR THOUSAND DOLLARS was paid
and received in full of all demands.

Thus after a persevering negotiation, conducted for
twelve years, at Washington, in the Chesapeake Bay,
at Bermuda, at London, and at Petersburgh, did our
Government succeed in obtaining most ample compensation for the fugitives.   Commissioners were
then appointed to distribute this sum ; and after fixing an average value on each slave proved to have
been carried away, it was found that a *surplus still
remained ;* and this surplus was divided among the
masters !

Having now seen the success that attended the
pursuit of fugitive slaves, let us next witness the

EFFORTS OF THE FEDERAL GOVERNMENT TO RECOVER
SHIPWRECKED SLAVES.

Considering the extent of the American slave-
trade, it is not surprising that our SLAVERS are occasionally driven out of their course ; and are sometimes wrecked upon the dangerous reefs abounding
in the neighboring Archipelago.

On the 3d January, 1831, the brig Comet, a regular
slaver from the District of Columbia, on her usual
voyage from Alexandria to New Orleans, with a cargo of 164 slaves, was lost off the Island of Abaco.
The slaves were saved, and carried into New Providence, where they were set at liberty by the authorities of the island.   A portion of the cargo, (146
head) was insured at New Orleans for $71,330.

On the 4th February, 1839, the brig Encomium, from
Charleston to New Orleans with 45 slaves, was also
wrecked near Abaco, and the slaves carried into New

Providence, where, like their predecessors, they were declared to be free.

In February, 1835, the Enterprise, another slaver from the National Domain, on her voyage to Charleston, with 78 slaves, was driven into Bermuda in distress. The passengers, instead of being thrown into prison, as Bermudians would have been in Charleston under similar circumstances, were hospitably treated, and permitted to go at large. These successive and unexpected transmutations of slaves into freemen, roused the ready zeal of the Federal Government. Directly on the loss of the Comet, instructions were sent from Washington to our Minister, to demand of the British Government the value of the cargo. In 1832, another despatch was forwarded on the subject. The instructions were again renewed in 1833 ; the Secretary of State remarking, this case " *must* be brought to a conclusion—the doctrine that would justify the liberation of our slaves, is too dangerous to a large section of our country to be tolerated."

In 1834, fresh instructions were sent, and a demand ordered to be made for the value of the slaves in the Encomium.

In 1835, similar instructions were sent relative to the Enterprise.

In 1836, the instructions were renewed ; the Secretary observing to Mr. Stevenson, " In the present state of our diplomatic relations with the Government of His Britannic Majesty, *the most immediately pressing* of the matters with which the United States' Legation at London is now charged, is the claim of certain American citizens against Great Britain for a number of slaves, the CARGOES of three vessels wrecked in British islands in the Atlantic."

From a long and labored commmunication from Mr. Stevenson to Lord Palmerston, we extract the following *morceau.*

" The undersigned feels assured that it will only be necessary to refer Lord Palmerston to the provisions of the Constitution of the United States, and the laws of many of the States, to satisfy him of the *existence* of slavery, and that slaves are there regarded and protected as property ; that by these laws, there is in fact *no distinction in principle between property in persons and property in things ; and that the Government have more than once, in the most solemn manner, determined that slaves killed in the service of the United States, even in a state of war, were to be regarded as property, and not as persons ; and the Government held responsible for their value."*

No answer having been vouchsafed to this letter, and the argument being exhausted, Mr. Stevenson tried the virtue of a diplomatic hint that the United States would go to war for their slaves ; expressing his hope in a letter to Lord Palmerston, that the British Government would " not longer consent to postpone the decision of a subject which had been for so many years under its consideration ; and the effect of which can be none other than to throw not only additional impediments in the way of an adjustment, and increase those feelings of dissatisfaction and irritation which have already been excited ; but by possibility tend to *disturb and weaken the kind and amicable relations which now so happily subsist between the two countries, and on the preservation of which, so essentially depend the interests and happiness of both."*
(Letter of 31st December, 1836.)

The British cabinet, after long delays, reluctantly consented to pay for the cargoes of the Comet and Encomium on the ground that at the time, the slaves composing them were liberated, slavery still existed in the British West Indies; but inasmuch as the emancipation Act had been passed before the arrival of the Enterprize, *her* passengers could not be recognized by British courts as property, and therefore the government could not and would not pay for them. The letter of Lord Palmerston announcing this determination concluded as follows : " Slavery being now abolished throughout the British empire, there can be no well-founded claim for compensation in respect of slaves who, under *any circumstances*, may come into British colonies, any more than there would be with respect to slaves brought into the United Kingdom."

This announcement was received in high dudgeon at Washington. Mr. Forsyth, the Secretary of State, wrote (27th March, 1837) to Mr. Stevenson, that the principles on which the claim of the owner of the slaves on board the Enterprize had been rejected, " are regarded by the PRESIDENT as inconsistent with the respect due from all foreign powers to the *institutions* of a friendly nation!' Mr. Van Buren it seems is yet to learn, that our republican institution of negro slavery, instead of being regarded with respect, is viewed with scorn and detestation by the civilized world. He is not, however, ignorant of the influence which *his* respect for it will have on the next presidential election. Mr. Forsyth proceeded :—" The soundness of the principle is explicitly denied, and the serious consequences with which, in the judgment of the PRESIDENT, it is fraught to the *property and*

7

tranquillity of our citizens, call imperatively upon HIM
to announce to his majesty's government, immediately
and solemnly, that its application to them *never can
be acquiesced in by the government of the United States.*"
. . . . " The PRESIDENT has been *particularly affected* by
the declaration, that no claim for slaves coming into
the British dominions, under àny circumstances, will
be entertained by his majesty's government. Although the President well knows that such is not the
intention of his majesty's government, yet this declaration, if not regarded as an invitation, will be the
strongest inducement to the flight òr abduction of
slaves, by fraud or force, from their masters ; and if
adhered to çannot fail to be considered, especially by
the sufferers from its influence, as an evidence of a
spirit hostile to the repose and security of the United
States." . . . . "Irritated by discussion without agreement, DISCUSSION WILL BE ABANDONED FOR RETALIATION
OR RETORTION ; and sooner or later the cordial good
will, at present so happily existing between the two
countries, will be converted into BITTER HOSTILITY—the
forerunner of incalculable injuries to both."

Mr. Stevenson was directed to lay this bullying
epistle " *in extenso*" before the British minister. Lòrd
Palmerston, in his reply, did not condescend to notice
the threats of Messrs. Van Buren and Forsyth, but
calmly *repeated* the assurance, that " Slavery being
now abolished throughout the British empire, there
can be no well-founded claim on the part of any fo-
reigner in respect of slaves who, under *any circumstances whatever*, may come into the British colonies,
any more than there would be in respect to slaves
who might come into the united kingdom."

The Federal Government did not deem it expedient, on the receipt of this despatch, to declare war against Great Britain, but preferred making another attempt at negotiation; and a most extraordinary attempt it was. Mr. Stevenson was instructed (12th March, 1838) to ascertain whether the British government "are prepared *at once* to enter upon the negotiation of a convention for regulating the disposition of-slaves belonging to the United States, that may be carried by force into the colonies lying contiguous to our territories, or driven in by stress of weather; with a view to the prevention of the ill effects to be apprehended from future collisions upon a subject so liable to produce in the people of the respective countries a high degree of excitement and irritation. In the *meantime*, the President, anxious to avoid every thing that might tend in the least degree to disturb the amicable relations subsisting between the two countries, WILL ABSTAIN from taking those steps for the security of the rights and property of our citizens which the recent decision of her majesty's government, in the absence of any agreement upon the subject, would render necessary, *until* opportunity is offered for *receiving the answer* of her majesty's government, to the application which you are hereby directed to make."

It would be doing injustice to Mr. Van Buren to suppose him capable of the weakness of believing that such a proposition would be listened to after the reiterated declarations to the contrary by Lord Palmerston. The correspondence it was known would be published before the next election; and the South would perceive that the President, although a northern man, had done what he could to sustain "the rights and property" of the slaveholders. A reprieve, it will be seen, was granted to her majesty's government until an opportunity was afforded for receiving its answer. On the 10th July, 1838, Mr. Stevenson laid before the British minister the terms of the required treaty, which were,—

1st. That Great Britain should "refrain from *forcing* liberty upon such American slaves" as might hereafter be compelled to enter British colonial ports.

2d. That she should prohibit the landing of such slaves in the colonies.

3d. That when unavoidably landed, they should be placed under *military* guard till their owners could re-ship them. The *answer*, big with the fate of Britain, and which was to terminate Mr. Van Buren's longsuffering and forbearance, was returned on the 10th July, 1838,—and such an answer! The American minister is assured that "an engagement on the part of Great Britain not to *force* liberty upon American slaves, would appear to assume a *preference* to slavery on the part of such persons which is scarcely consistent with the known principles of human nature;" and moreover, that such engagement is wholly unnecessary, since the British law forces no slave to leave a master he wishes to serve. But that a law, depriving American slaves in the British dominions of the right of habeas corpus, "would be so entirely at variance with every principle of the British Constitution, that *no government would venture to propose it to Parliament, and no Parliament would agree to adopt it.*" And as to placing American slaves under a military guard, that they might be restored to their masters, it would be a duty "*so repugnant to every feeling of the officers and men of the British army,* that her majesty's government would in any case be extremely unwilling to call upon her majesty's troops to perform it ; and, in the next place, it is doubtful whether the troops could be so employed consistently with the law now in force for the abolition of the slave trade, and her majesty's government could not propose to Parliament the *repeal of that law.*"

Such was the answer,—and not only has it been received, but it has been submitted to Congress ; and yet Mr. Van Buren still *abstains* "from taking those steps for the security of the rights and property of our citizens" which the decision of her majesty's government renders necessary !

Thus for eight successive years has the cabinet at Washington been sending instructions to their agents in England to procure payment for these cargoes of human flesh : nor have Congress been wanting in zeal on the same subject. *Twice* has the Senate called on the President to report the progress of the negotiation. The first call (7th February, 1837) asked for a copy of the " Correspondence with the Government of Great Britain in relation to the *outrage* committed on our flag, and the rights of our citizens, by the authorities of Bermuda and New Providence, in *seizing* the slaves on board the brigs ' Encomium' and ' Enterprize,' engaged in the *coasting trade*, but which were forced by shipwreck and stress of weather into the ports of those islands."

The language of this resolution indicates the influence exerted by slavery over the Federal Government. Should a murderer escape from England and land on our shores, we refuse to surrender him to the justice of his country ; but when the West India authorities

7*

refuse to deliver two hundred and eighty-seven innocent men, women, and children, thrown by the tem-
pest under their protection, into hopeless intermina-
ble slavery, the Senate solemnly pronounce the refusal to be an *outrage* on our flag, and the rights of our
citizens. Moreover, the liberation of these persons
is spoken of as a *seizure* of them, and the *slavers* carrying human cargoes to market, are most audaciously
declared to have been engaged in the *coasting trade !*
The real trade in which these vessels were engaged,
was

THE AMERICAN SLAVE TRADE UNDER THE PROTECTION AND REGULATION OF THE FEDERAL GOVERNMENT.

We shall first exhibit the character and extent of
this trade, and then show that it is in fact carried on
under the protection and regulation of the Federal
Government.

The competition of free with slave labor in the
bread stuffs and some other productions of Maryland,
Virginia, and North Carolina, have greatly reduced
the value of slaves as laborers in those States; and
hence the disposition manifested there some years
since, to get rid of this unprofitable portion of their
population. But the rapid extension of the cotton
and sugar cultivation in the extreme South, together
with the settlement of the new States of Alabama,
Mississippi, Missouri, and Arkansas, occasioned a prodigious demand for slaves; and the agriculturists of
Virginia and the neighboring states discovered that
their most lucrative occupation was that of raising
live stock for the southern and western markets. In

Georgia and South Carolina it has also been found more advantageous to export their supernumeraries to Mobile, New Orleans, or Natchez, than to employ them on their well-stocked plantations. Hence has grown up an almost incredible transfer of slaves from the North to the South; and recently a new market has been opened in Texas, giving an additional stimulus to the trade. It is impossible to ascertain the exact amount of this trade, as the Secretary of the Treasury in his annual report on the commercial statistics of the United States, has never included any statements respecting this branch of the "coasting trade." But, indeed, the returns from the several Custom-Houses of the size and value of the human cargoes cleared for the southern ports, if given, would afford a very inadequate idea of the extent of the traffic, since it is carried on by land as well as by sea. Whole coffles of chained slaves are driven long and painful journeys in the interior of the Republic, much in the same manner as in the wilds of Africa. The Rev. Mr. Dickey, in a published letter thus describes a coffle he met on the road in Kentucky :—"I discovered about forty black men all chained together in the following manner : each of them was handcuffed, and they were arranged in rank and file ; a chain perhaps forty feet long was stretched between two ranks, to which short chains were joined, which connected with the handcuffs. Behind them were, I suppose, *thirty women* in double rank, *the couples tied hand to hand.*"

The Presbyterian Synod of Kentucky, in an address, in 1835, to the churches under their care, speaking of this trade, say,

"Brothers and sisters, parents and children, hus-

bands and wives, are torn asunder, and permitted to
see each other no more. These acts are *daily* occur-
ing in the midst of us. The shrieks and agony often
witnessed on such occasions, proclaim with a trumpet
tongue the iniquity of OUR system. There is not a
neighborhood where these heart-rending scenes are
not displayed. *There is not a village or road* that
does not behold the sad procession of *manacled* out-
casts, whose mournful countenances tell that they
are exiled by force from all that their hearts hold
dear."

J. K. PAULDING, the present Secretary of the Navy,
gives the following picture of a scene he witnessed
in Virginia :

" The sun was shining out very hot, and in turning
an angle of the road we encountered the following
group : first, a little cart drawn by one horse, in
which five or six half naked black children were
tumbled like pigs together. The cart had no cover-
ing, and they seemed to have been actually broiled
to sleep. Behind the cart marched three black women, with head, neck and breasts, uncovered, and
without shoes or stockings ; next came three men,
bareheaded, half naked, and *chained together with an
ox chain*. Last of all came a white man—a white
man, Frank !—on horseback, carrying pistols in his
belt, and who, as we passed him, had the impudence
to look us in the face without blushing. I should
like to have seen him hunted by blood-hounds. At
a house where we stopped, a little further on, we
learned that he had bought these miserable beings in
Maryland, and was marching them in this manner to
some of the more southern States. Shame on the

State of Maryland!—I say—and shame on the State of Virginia! and every State through which this wretched cavalcade was permitted to pass. Do they expect that such exhibitions will not dishonor them in the eyes of strangers, however they may be reconciled to them by education and habit ?"*

* " Letters from the South, written during an excursion in the summer of 1816." New York, 1817. Vol. I. Letter XI. p. 117.

It may be thought by some that the elevation to a seat in the Cabinet, of a gentleman who expresses himself with so much warmth and fearlessness against one of the " peculiar institutions of the South," militates against our idea that the influence of the Federal Government is exerted in behalf of slavery. Singular as it may appear, the appointment of Mr. Paulding is nevertheless strongly corroborative of the opinion we have advanced ; and the explanation is at once easy and amusing. The " Letters from the South" were reprinted in 1835, and form the fifth and sixth volumes of an edition of " Paulding's Works." The letter from which we have quoted consists of fourteen pages, devoted to the subject of slavery. On turning to the corresponding letter in the *recent* edition we find it shrunk to *three* pages, containing no allusion to the internal trade, nor anything else that could offend the most sensitive southerner. In the nineteenth letter, as printed in 1817, there is not a word about slavery. In the same letter, as published in 1835, we meet with the following most wonderful *prediction;* a prediction that has lately been cited in the newspapers as a proof of the sagacity and foresight of the Secretary of the Navy :—

" The second cause of disunion will be found in the slave population of the South, *whenever* the misguided, or wilfully malignant zeal of the advocates of emancipation, shall institute, *as it one day doubtless will,* a crusade against the constitutional rights of the slave owners, by sending among them fanatical agents and fanatical tracts, calculated to render the slaves disaffected, and the situation of the master and his family dangerous ; when appeals shall be made under the sanction of religion to the passions of these ignorant and excited blacks, calculated and intended to rouse their worst and most dangerous passions, and to place the

The annexed picture, it will be perceived, is drawn
by a *southern* pencil. "Place·yourself in imagination
for a moment in their condition—with *heavy galling
chains* riveted upon your person, *half. naked, half
starved,* your back *lacerated* with the knotted whip,
travelling to a region where your condition through
time will be second only to the wretched creatures
in hell. This depiction is not visionary—would to
God that it was!" *Editorial, Maryville (Tennessee)
Intelligencer,* 4th *October,* 1835.

As we are about to enter into particulars respecting the American slave trade, it may not be uninteresting to inquire who are its victims? They are
native born Americans. But of what color and descent? This will no doubt be deemed by many a
very unnecessary question; and no little indignation

very lives of their masters, their wives, and their children in the
deepest peril; *when societies are formed* in the sister States for the
avowed purpose of virtually destroying the value of this principal
item in the property of a southern planter; when it becomes a
question mooted in the legislatures of the States, or of the general government, whether the rights of the master over his slave
shall be any longer recognized or maintained, and when it is at
last evident that nothing will preserve them but secession, then
will certain of the stars of our beautiful constellation "start madly
from their spheres and jostle the others in their wild career."

In the title of the new edition, the *date* of the "excursion" is
modestly omitted, but the reader is not informed that the spirit of
prophecy descended upon the writer, not while journeying at the
South, but while witnessing in New York the operations of *the
predicted* societies, and *after* the city had been convulsed by the
abolition riots.

In 1836, Mr. Paulding published his "Slavery in the United
States." In this work both the Old and New Testament are
made to give their sanction to slavery. Great Britain, in abolishing slavery in the West Indies, is charged with having "commit-

will probably be excited when we answer that large numbers of these victims are *white* men and women, and the *children of American citizens.*

People at the North are disposed to be incredulous, when they hear of *white* slaves at the South; and yet a little reflection would convince them not only that there must be such slaves under the present system, but that in process of time, a large proportion of the slaves must be as white as their masters. Were there no other sources of information respecting the complexions of the southern slaves, the newspaper notices of runaways would most abundantly confirm our assertion. Of these notices, we give the following as samples.

" $100 *Reward.*—The above reward will be paid for the apprehension of my man William. He is

ted robbery under cover of humanity."—(p. 51.) "A community of free blacks rising among the ruins of States, lords of the soil, smoking with the habitations and blood of their exterminated masters and families," would, we are assured, be only fulfilling "the wishes" of the abolitionists.—(p. 56.) The advocates of immediate emancipation recommend, it is asserted, "indiscriminate marriages between the whites and blacks;"—(p. 61.) and well educated respectable females amongst them are apparently anxious "to become the mothers of mulattoes."—(p. 62.) Slavery, we are told, "is becoming gradually divested of all its harsh features, and is now only the bugbear of the imagination;—(p. 26.) and Mr. Paulding affirms—"In a residence of several years within the District, and a pretty extensive course of travel in some of the southern States, (the excursion in the summer of 1816, we suppose,) we never saw or heard of any such instances of cruelty. *We saw no chains* (!) and heard no stripes."—(p. 168.)

We trust our readers are now fully convinced of this gentleman's qualifications for the office of Secretary of the Navy, and of Mr. Van Buren's consistency in appointing him.

a very bright mulatto—*straight yellowish hair*. I have no doubt he will change his name, and try to pass himself for a WHITE MAN, which he may be able to do, unless to a close observer.
August 9."   T. S. PICHARD.

" $100 *Reward*.—Ranaway from James Hyhart, Paris, Kentucky, on the 29th June last, the mulatto boy Norton, about fifteen years, a very bright mulatto, and would be taken for a WHITE BOY, if not closely examined. His hair is black and *straight*, &c."—*New Orleans True American*, 11*th August* 1836.

" $100 *Reward*—Will be given for the apprehension of my negro (!) Edmund Kenney. He has *straight* hair, and complexion so nearly WHITE, that it is believed a stranger would suppose *there was no African blood in him*. He was with my boy Dick a short time since in Norfolk, *and offered him for sale*, and was apprehended, but escaped under pretence of being a WHITE MAN.
ANDERSON BOWLES.
Richmond Whig, 6*th January*, 1836."

" $50 *Reward* will be given for the apprehension and delivery to me of the following slaves : Samuel, and Judy his wife with their four children, belonging to the estate of Sacker Dubberly, deceased.
I will give $10 for the apprehension of William Dubberly, a slave belonging to the estate. William is about 19 years old, QUITE WHITE, and would not readily be mistaken for a slave.
JOHN T. LANE.
Newbern Spectator, 13th *March*, 1837."

" $100 *Reward.*—Ranaway from the subscriber, a bright mulatto man slave, named Sam. *Light sandy hair, blue eyes, ruddy complexion*—is so WHITE as very easily to pass for a free WHITE MAN.

EDWIN PECK.

Mobile, April 22, 1837."

" $50 *Reward.*—I will give the above reward of fifty dollars for the apprehension and securing in any jail, so that I get him again, or delivering to me in Dandridge, E. Tenn., my mulatto boy, named Preston, about twenty years old. It is supposed he will try to pass as a *free* WHITE MAN. *Oct.* 12, 1838." JOHN ROPER.

" *Ranaway* from the subscriber, working on the plantation of Col. H. Tinker, a bright mulatto boy, named Alfred. Alfred is about 18 years of age, pretty well grown, has *blue eyes, light flaxen hair, skin disposed to freckle.* He will try to pass as FREE BORN.

S. G. STEWART.

Green County, Alabama."

In the *New Orleans Bee,* of June 22, 1831, P. BAHI dvertises as a runaway, "Maria, with a CLEAR WHITE complexion!"

Mr. Paxton, a Virginia writer, tells us in his work on slavery, that "the best blood in Virginia flows in the veins of the slaves."

Dr Torrey, in his work on domestic slavery in the United States, p. 14, says: "While at a public house in Fredericktown, there came into the bar-room, on Sunday, a decently dressed white man, of quite a light complexion, in company with one who was to-

8

tally black. After they went away, the landlord observed that the *white man* was a slave. I asked him with some surprise how that could be possible? To which he replied, that he was a descendant, by female ancestry, of an African slave. He also stated, that not far from Fredericktown, there was a slave estate on which there were several *white* females, of as fair and elegant appearance as white ladies in general, held in legal bondage as *slaves ! !*"

A Missouri paper, reporting the trial of a *slave boy,* remarks: " All the physiological marks of distinction which characterize the African descent, had disappeared. His skin was *fair,* his hair soft, straight, fine and white, his eyes blue, but rather disposed to the hazel-nut color, nose prominent, the lips small and well formed, forehead high and prominent."

In the summer of 1835, a slaveholder from Maryland arrested as his fugitive, a young woman in Philadelphia. A trial ensued, when it was most conclusively proved that the alleged slave, Mary Gilmore, was the child of poor *Irish* parents, and had not a drop of African blood in her veins.

A paper printed at Louisville, Ky., the " Emporium," relates a circumstance that occurred in that city, in the following terms. " A laudable indignation was universally manifested among our citizens on Saturday last, by the exposure of a woman and two children for sale at public auction, at the front of our principal tavern. The woman and children were as WHITE as any of our citizens; indeed, we scarcely ever saw a child with a fairer or clearer complexion than the younger one."—*Niles' Register, June,* 1821.

Mr. Niles tells us, in his Register, that Mr. Calhoun, the late Vice President, had related to him the case of a man "placed on the stand for sale as a slave, whose appearance, in *all respects*, gave him a better claim to the character of a WHITE MAN, than most persons so acknowledged could show."— *Register*, 25th *Oct.* 1834.

We will now attempt to give the reader some idea of the *extent* of the trade—a trade in which human beings of every shade, from the purest white to the deepest black, are made articles of merchandize, and treated with cruelty little if any less than that which has made the African slave-trade the execration of the civilized world.

"Dealing in slaves," says the Baltimore Register, "has become a large business; establishments are made in several places in Maryland and Virginia, at which they are sold like cattle: these places of deposit are strongly built, and well supplied with iron thumb-screws and gags, and ornamented with cow-skins and other whips, oftentimes bloody."

The advertisements of the Baltimore traders show that the Maryland Colonization Society, in their endeavors to suppress the slave trade, may find a field for their labors less distant than the Coast of Africa. We annex some samples.

" *Austin Woodfolk*, of Baltimore, wishes to inform the slaveholders of Maryland and Virginia, that their friend still lives to give cash and the highest price for negroes," &c.

" *General Slave Agency Office.*—Gentlemen planters

from the South and others who wish to purchase negroes, would do well to give me a call.

LEWIS SCOTT."

"*Cash for two hundred Negroes.*—The highest cash prices will be paid for negroes of both sexes, by application to me or my agent, at Booth's Garden.

HOPE H. SLATER."

"*For New-Orleans.*—A copperea, copper-fastened packet-brig Isaac Franklin, will sail on the 1st Feb. for Baltimore. *Those having servants to ship* will do well by making early application to James F. Purvis," &c

Human flesh is now the great staple of Virginia. In the Legislature of this State, in 1832, THOMAS JEFFERSON RANDOLPH declared that Virginia had been converted into " *one grand menagerie, where men are reared for the market like oxen for the shambles.*" This same gentleman thus compared the foreign with the domestic traffic. " The trader (African) receives the slaves, a stranger in aspect, language, and manner, from the merchant who brought him from the interior. But *here*, sir, individuals whom the master has known from infancy—whom he has seen sporting in the innocent gambols of childhood — who have been accustomed to look to him for protection, *he tears from the mother's arms, and sells into a strange country, among a strange people, subject to cruel task-masters.* In my opinion it is *much worse.*"

MR. GHOLSON, of Virginia, in his speech in the Legislature of that State, January 18, 1831, (see Richmond Whig,) says. " The legal maxim of *partus sequitur ventrem*, is coeval with the existence of the rights of property itself, and is founded in wisdom and justice. It is only on the justice and inviolability of this maxim, that the master foregoes the service of the female slave, has her nursed and attended during the period of her gestation,.and raises the helpless and infant offspring. The value of the property justifies the expense; and I do not hesitate to say, that *in its increase consists much of our wealth.*"

PROFESSOR DEW, now President of the College of William and Mary, Virginia, in his review of the debate in the Virginia Legislature, 1831–2, speaking of the revenue arising from the trade, says, "A full equivalent being thus left in the place of the slave, this emigration becomes an advantage to the State, and does not check the black population as much as at first view we might imagine, because it furnishes every inducement to the master to attend to the negroes, to ENCOURAGE BREEDING, and *to cause the greatest number possible to be raised.* * * Virginia is, in fact, a NEGRO-RAISING STATE for other States."

Mr. C. F. MERCER asserted in the Virginia Convention of 1829, " The tables of the natural growth of the slave population demonstrate, when compared with the increase of its numbers in the Commonwealth for twenty years past, that an annual revenue of not less than a *million and a half of dollars* is derived from the *exportation* of a part of this population."—*Debates*, p. 99.

Professor E. A Andrews gives a conversation he had with a trader on board a steam-boat on the Potomac, in 1835. " In selling his slaves, N——— assures me he never separates families; but that in

8*

purchasing them he is often compelled to do so, for that his business is to purchase, and he must take such as are in the market. Do you often buy the wife without the husband? Yes, very often; and frequently, too, they sell me the mother, while they keep the children. I have often known them take *away the infant from the mother's breast, and keep it, while they sold her.* Children from one to eighteen months old, are now worth about one hundred dollars."*

The town of Petersburg, in Virginia, seems to enjoy a large share of this commerce, judging from the advertisements of its merchants.

" *Cash for Negroes.*—The subscribers are particularly anxious to make a *shipment* of negroes shortly. All persons who have slaves to part with, will do well to call as soon as possible. OVERLY & SAUNDERS."

" The subscriber being desirous of making *another shipment* by the Brig Adelaide, to New Orleans, on the first of March, will give a good market price for fifty negroes, from *ten* to thirty years old.
HENRY DAVIS."

" The subscriber wishes to purchase *one hundred slaves,* of both sexes, from the age of *ten* to thirty, for which he is disposed to give much higher prices than have heretofore been given. He will call on those living in the adjacent counties to see any *property.*   ANSLEY DAVIS."

* Slavery and the Domestic Slave Trade in the United States, p. 147.

But of all the Virginia merchants, Mr. Collier, of Richmond, seems to be the most enterprising. We give extracts from his

"*Notice.*—This is to inform my former acquaintances, and the public generally, that I yet continue in the SLAVE TRADE, *at Richmond, Virginia,* and will at all times buy and give a fair market price for *young negroes.* Persons in this State, Maryland, or North Carolina, wishing to sell lots of negroes, are particularly requested to forward their wishes to me at this place. Persons wishing to purchase lots of negroes, are requested to give me a call, as I keep constantly on hand at this place, *a great many* for sale ; and have at this time the use of one hundred young negroes, consisting of boys, young men, and girls. I will sell at all times, at a small advance on cost, to suit purchasers. I have comfortable rooms, with a *jail* attached, for the reception of the negroes ; and persons coming to this place to sell slaves, can be accommodated, and every attention necessary will be given to have them well attended to ; and when it may be desired, the reception of the company of *gentlemen dealing in slaves,* will conveniently and attentively be received. My situation is very healthy and suitable for the business. LEWIS A. COLLIER."

Joseph Wood, of Hamburg, South Carolina, a "gentleman dealing in slaves," advertises that he "has on hand a likely parcel of *Virginia negroes,* and receives new supplies *every fifteen days.*"

" 120 *Negroes for sale.*—The subscriber has just arrived *from Petersburg, Virginia,* with one hundred

and twenty likely young negroes, of both sexes, and
every description, which he offers for sale on the
most reasonable terms. The lot now on hand, consists of plough-boys, several likely and well qualified
house servants, of both sexes, several women with
small children, *small girls*, suitable for nurses, and
several SMALL BOYS WITHOUT THEIR MOTHERS.

BENJAMIN DAVIS."

Hamburg, S. C., Sept. 28, 1838.

And what are the pecuniary results of this commerce ? Mr. Mercer, as we have seen, estimated the
annual revenue to Virginia from the export of human
flesh, at *one million and a half of dollars.* But this
was in 1829, before the trade had reached its present
palmy state. " The Virginia Times," in 1836, in an
article on the importance of increasing the banking
capital of the Commonwealth, estimates the number
of slaves exported for sale the " last twelve months,"
at FORTY THOUSAND ; each slave averaging six hundred dollars, and thus yielding a capital of TWENTY-
FOUR MILLIONS, of which the Editor thinks, at least
thirteen millions might be contributed for banking
purposes.*

In 1837, a committee, appointed at a public meeting of the citizens of Mobile, on the subject of the
existing pecuniary pressure, in their report stated :
" that so large has been the return of slave labor,
that purchases by Alabama, of that species of property from other States since 1833, have amounted to
TEN MILLIONS OF DOLLARS ANNUALLY."

Let us now visit the " Metropolis of the Nation,"

* Niles's Register.

the very heart of this mighty commerce in the bodies and souls of men. The District of Columbia, from its relative situation to the breeding States, forms a convenient depôt for the negroes, previous to their exportation; and the non-interference of Congress, gives the traders " under the exclusive jurisdiction" of the Federal Government, as unlimited power over the treatment and stowage of their human cargoes, as their brethren enjoy, on the coast of Guinea.

Hence large establishments have grown up upon the national domain, provided with prisons for the safe-keeping of the negroes till a full cargo is procured; and should at any time the factory prisons be insufficient, the public ones, erected by Congress, are at the service of the dealers, and the United States Marshal becomes the agent of the slave trader !

It must be admitted, that the following pictures of the scenes witnessed in the District of Columbia, are drawn by impartial hands. So long ago as 1802, the grand jury of Alexandria, complaining of the trade, remarked: " These dealers in the persons of our fellow-men, collect within this district from various parts, numbers of these victims of slavery, and lodge them in some place of confinement until they have completed their numbers. They are then turned out into our streets, and exposed to view *loaded with chains*, as though they had committed some heinous offence against our laws. We consider it as a grievance that citizens from a distant part of the United States, should be permitted to come within the District, and pursue a traffic fraught with so much misery to a class of beings entitled to our protection, by the laws of justice and humanity ; and that the in-

terposition of civil authority cannot be had to prevent
parents being wrested from their offspring, and children from their parents, without respect to the ties of
nature. We consider these grievances demanding
legislative redress"—that is, redress by Congress.

In 1816, Judge Morell of the Circuit Court of the
United States, in his charge to the Grand Jury of
Washington, observed, speaking of the slave trade :
" The frequency with which the streets of the city
had been *crowded with manacled captives*, sometimes
on the Sabbath, could not fail to shock the feelings of
all humane persons."

The same year, JOHN RANDOLPH moved in the House
of Representatives for a committee " to inquire into
the existence of an inhuman and illegal traffic of
slaves carried on, in, and through the District of Columbia, and report whether any or what measures
are necessary for putting a stop to the same." The
motion was adopted ; had it been made twenty years
later, it would under the rules of the House, have
been laid on the table, " and no further action had
thereon."

The Alexandria Gazette of June 22d, 1827, thus
describes the scenes sanctioned by our professedly
republican and Christian Legislature : " scarcely a
week passes without some of these wretched creatures being driven through our streets. After having
been confined, and sometimes manacled in a loathsome prison, they are turned out in public view to
take their departure for the South. The children and
some of the women are generally crowded into a cart
or wagon, while others follow on foot, not unfrequently *handcuffed and chained together*. Here you

may behold fathers and brothers leaving behind them the dearest objects of affection, and moving slowly along in the mute agony of despair—there the young mother sobbing over the infant whose innocent smiles seem but to increase her misery. · From some you will hear the burst of bitter lamentation, while from others, the loud hysteric laugh breaks forth, denoting still deeper agony."

In 1828, a petition for the suppression of this trade was presented to Congress, signed by more than *one thousand inhabitants of this District.*

In 1829, the Grand Jury of Washington made a communication to Congress, in which they say, "Provision ought to be made to prevent purchasers, for the purpose of removal and transportation, from making the cities of the District, depôts for the *imprisonment* of the slaves they collect. The manner in which they are brought and confined in these places, *and carried through our streets*, is necessarily such as to excite the most painful feelings. It is believed that the whole community would be gratified by the *interference of Congress* for the suppression of these receptacles, and the exclusion of this *disgusting traffic* from the District."

In 1830, the "Washington Spectator" thus gave vent to its indignation.

"*The slave trade in the Capital.*—Let it be known to the citizens of America, that at the very time when the procession which contained the President of the United States and his cabinet was marching in triumph to the Capitol, another kind of procession was marching another way; and that consisted of colored human beings, *handcuffed in pairs*, and driven along by what had the appearance of a man on horseback! A similar scene was repeated on Saturday last; a drove, consisting of males and females, *chained in couples*, starting from Roly's tavern on foot for Alexandria, where with others they are to embark on board a slave ship in waiting to convey them to the South. Where is the O'Connell in this Republic that will plead for the emancipation of the District of Columbia?"

The advertisements of the dealers indicate the *extent* of the traffic. The National Intelligencer of the 28th March, 1836, printed at Washington, contained the following advertisements.

"*Cash for five hundred Negroes*, including both sexes, from *ten* to twenty-five years of age. Persons having likely servants to dispose of, will find it their interest to give us a call, as we will give higher prices in cash than any other purchaser who is now or may hereafter come into the MARKET.

FRANKLIN & AMFIELD, Alexandria."

"*Cash for three hundred Negroes.*—The highest cash price will be given by the subscriber, for negroes of both sexes, from the ages of twelve to twenty-eight.

WILLIAM H. WILLIAMS, Washington."

"*Cash for four hundred Negroes*, including both sexes, from twelve to twenty-five years of age.

JAMES H. BIRCH, Washington City."

"*Cash for Negroes.*—We will at all times give the highest prices in cash for likely young negroes of both sexes, from ten to thirty years of age.

J. W. NEAL & Co., Washington."

Here we find three traders in the District, advertising in one day for *twelve hundred* negroes, and a fourth offering to buy an indefinite number.

In a later number of the Intelligencer, we find the following.

" *Cash for Negroes.*—I will give the highest price for likely negroes from ten to twenty-five years of age.

GEORGE KEPHART."

" *Cash for Negroes.*—I will give cash and liberal prices for ANY number of young and likely negroes, from *eight* to forty years of age. Persons having negroes to dispose of will find it to their advantage to give me a call at my residence on the corner of Seventh-street and Maryland Avenue, and opposite Mr. William's *private jail.* WILLIAM H. RICHARDS."

" *Cash for Negroes.*—The subscriber wishes to purchase a number of negroes for the *Louisiana and Mississippi market.* Himself or an agent at all times can be found at *his jail,* on Seventh-street.

WM. H. WILLIAMS."

The unhappy beings purchased by these traders in human flesh, men and women, and children of *eight* years old, are sent to the South, either over land in coffles, or by sea, in crowded slavers. Fostered by Congress, these traders lose all sense of shame; and we have in the National Intelligencer the following announcement of the regular departure of *three slavers,* belonging to a single factory.

" *Alexandria and New Orleans Packets.*—Brig *Tri-*

bune, Samuel C. Bush, master, will sail as above on
the 1st January—Brig *Isaac Franklin,* Wm. Smith,
master, on the 15th January—Brig *Uncas,* Nath.
Boush, master, on the 1st February. They will continue to leave this port on the 1st and 15th of each
month, throughout the shipping season. *Servants
that are intended to be shipped, will at any time be received for safe-keeping at twenty-five cents a day.*

JOHN AMFIELD, Alexandria."

This infamous advertisement of the regular sailing
of three slavers, and the offer of the use of the factory prison, appears in one of the principal journals of
the United States. Its proprietor has several times
been chosen printer to Congress, and there is no reason for believing that he has ever lost the vote of a
northern member for this prostitution of his columns.

But the climax of infamy is still untold. This
trade in blood; this buying, imprisoning, and export-
ing of boys and girls eight years old; this tearing
asunder of husbands and wives, parents and children,
is all legalized *in virtue of authority delegated by Congress!!* The 249th page of the laws of the city of
Washington, is polluted by the following enactment,
bearing date 28th July, 1838.

" For a LICENSE to trade or traffic in slaves for profit,
four hundred dollars."

A terrific feature of this trade is the mortality it
occasions. A writer in the New Orleans Argus of 1830,
in an article on the sugar cultivation, thus coolly estimates one item of expenditure. " The loss by death
in bringing slaves from a northern climate, which our
planters are under the necessity of doing, is not less

than TWENTY-FIVE PER CENT." If the change of climate be thus fatal, then those who survive this change, must, of course, be deemed more valuable, as the planters will run less hazard in buying them after having become *acclimated*. Now what language do southern advertisements hold on this point? We have of course room for only a few *specimens*—but they attest the superior value attached to acclimated negroes, and of course the loss of life attributed to " bringing slaves from a northern climate."

" I offer my plantation for sale. Also seventy-five *acclimated negroes*. O. B. Cobb.
Vicksburg Register, Dec. 27, 1838."

"I will sell my Old River plantation, near Columbia, in Arkansas, also *one hundred and thirty acclimated negroes*. Ben. Hughes.
Port Gibson, 14th Jan."

" Probate sale.—Will be offered for sale at public auction to the highest bidder *one hundred and thirty acclimated slaves*. G. W. Keeton,
Judge of the Parish of Concordia, La.
March 22, 1837."

General Felix Houston advertises in the *Natchez Courier*, April 6th, 1838. " Thirty very fine *acclimated* negroes."

But the waste of life in the process of acclimation, is but a portion of the mortality caused by this murderous traffic. If we call to mind the crowded slavers—the chained coffles—the dreary journies of

hundreds of miles—the forced separation of husbands
and wives—parents and children—the broken hearts
and fevered brains of the helpless victims, we cannot
question that the sufferings of multitudes are short-
ened by a premature death. We could detail various
suicides, induced by the horrible anticipation of this
loathsome transfer—but one shall suffice, and that related by the present SECRETARY OF THE NAVY. This
gentleman, in his southern excursion, fell in company
with a coffle-driver, and in the *first* (not the last) edi-
tions of his letters from the South, gives the confes-
sions made by the wretch himself in his presence.

" All along the road, it seems, he made it his business to inquire where lived a man who might be
tempted to become a party in this *accursed traffic ;*
and when he had got some half dozen of these poor
creatures, *he tied their hands behind their backs*, and
drove them three or four hundred miles or more, bareheaded and half naked, through the burning southern
sun. ' I made one bad purchase though,' continued
he, ' I bought a young mulatto girl, a lively creature,
a great bargain. She had been the favorite of her
master, who had lately married. The difficulty was
to get her to go, for the poor creature loved her master. However, I swore most bitterly I was only going
to take her to her mother's, at ——, and she went
with me, though she seemed to doubt me very much.
But when she discovered, at last, that we were out of
the State, I thought she would go mad, and, in fact,
the next night she drowned herself in the river
close by. I lost a good five hundred dollars by this
foolish trick.' "—(Vol. I. p. 121.)*

* It was not, it would seem, till the honorable Secretary turned

We now put it to the consciences of our readers, if the facts developed in the preceding pages, do not amply justify the following pregnant remarks of the Editor of a late New Orleans Journal :

"The United States law (prohibiting the African slave trade,) may, and probably does put MILLIONS into the pockets of the people living between the Roanoke and Mason and Dixon's line ; still we think it would require some casuistry to show that the present slave trade from that quarter *is a whit better than the one from Africa.*"—*New Orleans Courier*, 15*th Feb.* 1839.

Such is the character and extent of the American slave trade, impudently and wickedly called by the Senate, " the coasting trade,"—a trade protected and regulated by the very government which in the Treaty of Ghent, with wonderful assurance, declared that " the traffic in slaves is irreconcileable with the principles of justice and humanity."

The government may be fairly said to protect the trade, when it refuses to exercise its constitutional power to suppress it. The very fact that slave traders are *licensed in the District*, is a full and complete acknowledgment that there is authority competent to forbid their nefarious business. The continuance of the traffic under the immediate and " exclusive jurisdiction" of the National Government, stamps with sin and disgrace every member of Congress who assents to it ; and more especially, and with peculiar infamy, those northern members who, for party purposes, vote

politician, that he discovered that slavery is now "only the bugbear of the imagination."

9*

that " Congress ought not in *any way* to interfere with slavery in the District of Columbia."

But we are constantly told by the apologists of slavery that the American slave trade is beyond the constitutional control of the Federal Government; yet that government abolished the *African* slave trade, and no human being ever questioned its right to do so ? But whence was that right derived ? Solely from the 8th Sec. of the 1st Art. of the Constitution, viz :—

" Congress shall have power to regulate commerce with foreign nations, and among the several States."

In virtue of this delegation of power, Congress has made it a capital crime to carry on commerce in *African* slaves. Now that this legislative prohibition of the traffic is constitutional, is proved by the highest possible authority, even the Constitution itself; for that instrument, after giving Congress power to regulate commerce with foreign nations, *restricts it* from abolishing the African slave trade before the expiration of twenty years.* To *regulate*, we are told, does not include the power to destroy;

* The phraseology of this restriction shows that it was intended to limit the power to regulate commerce as well " among the several States" as with foreign nations. " The *migration*, or importation of such person as any of the existing States shall think proper to admit, shall not be prohibited by the Congress prior to the year one thousand eight hundred and eight."—(Art. 1. Sec. 9.) If any State should think proper to admit slaves *migrating* from another State, it was not to be restrained from doing so till 1808. If it should think proper to *import* slaves from a foreign country, it might do so, notwithstanding the wishes of Congress, till the same period.

yet it seems the power to regulate commerce with foreign nations does include the power to interdict an odious, cruel, and wicked branch of it. By what logic then will it be shown that the power to regulate the commerce among the several States, does not include the power to interdict a traffic, in men, women, and children ? Is it more wicked, more base, more cruel, to traffic in African savages than in native born Americans—in WHITE men, and women, and children—in the offspring of our own citizens, and not unfrequently, of very distinguished citizens ? Yet it is this abominable commerce that our government fosters and protects. We have seen its watchful guardianship over this trade in its unceasing endeavors to obtain compensation from Great Britain for 287 slaves thrown by the winds and waves under her protection. Mr. Van Buren, our Minister in England, in an official note on this subject, (Feb. 25, 1832,) remarked :—

" The Government of the United States respecting the actual and unavoidable condition of things at home, while it most sedulously and rigorously guards against the further introduction of slaves, *protects* at the same time by reasonable laws the rights of the owners of that species of property in the States where it exists, and *permits* its transfer coastwise from one of these States to another, under suitable restrictions to prevent the fraudulent introduction of foreign slaves."

By the act of Congress of 2d March, 1807, masters of vessels under 40 tons burden, are forbidden to transport coastwise from one port to another in the United States any person of color to be sold or held as a slave, under the penalty of $800 for each slave so transported.

By the same Act masters of vessels, over 40 ιuns burden, sailing coastwise from one port to another, and *intending to transport persons of color to be sold or held as slaves*, must first make out duplicate manifests, specifying the names, age, sex, and stature, of the persons transported, and the names and residence of their owner or shipper. These manifests are to be delivered to the collector of the port who is to retain one, and return the other to the master with " *a permit*," endorsed on it, " authorizing him to proceed to the port of destination." If the master presumes to transport a slave without such permit, not only is the vessel forfeited, but the master is to pay a penalty of $1000 for each slave shipped. On the arrival of the vessel at the port of destination, the manifest, with the permit, is to be handed to the collector, who thereupon is to grant a " *permit*" for the landing of the slaves, and if any are landed without such permit, the master forfeits one thousand dollars. So it seems Congress may prohibit the slave trade in vessels *under* forty tons; but according to northern politicians, it would be unconstitutional to prohibit it in vessels *over* forty tons; and according to the slaveholders, such a prohibition would cause the dissolution of the Union! But alas! the permission, regulation, and protection of this traffic is in perfect keeping with

THE DUPLICITY OF THE FEDERAL GOVERNMENT IN REGARD TO THE SUPPRESSION OF THE AFRICAN SLAVE TRADE.

The great struggle for the abstract principles of human liberty, in which our fathers engaged with so much zeal, had, at the close of the revolutionary war, excited a very general conviction of the injustice of slavery. When the convention appointed to form a Federal Constitution assembled, the northern and many of the southern delegates were disposed to give the new government such unqualified power over the commerce of the nation, as would enable it to abolish a traffic no less at variance with our republican professions than with the precepts of humanity and religion. A portion of the southern delegates, however, insisted on a temporary restriction of this power as the price of their adhesion to the Union; and their threat of marring the beauty, symmetry, and strength of the fair fabric about to be erected, by withdrawing from it the support of the States they represented, unfortunately induced the convention to yield to their wishes, and to insert in the Constitution a clause restraining Congress from abolishing the African slave trade for twenty years. Mr. Madison has left us the following history of this iniquitous clause. " The southern States would not have entered into the union of America without the temporary permission of that trade. The gentlemen from South Carolina and Georgia argued in this manner—' We have now liberty to import this species of property, and much of the property now possessed has been purchased, or otherwise acquired in contemplation of improving it by the

assistance of imported slaves. What would be the
consequence of hindering us from it ? The slaves of
Virginia would rise in value, and we should be obliged
to go to your markets.' "—*Debates in Virginia Convention.*

We have here the solution of much contradictory
action on the part of slaveholders in regard to this
trade. It seems to have been early discovered that its
abolition would be advantageous to the slave-breeders,
but not to the slave-buyers. Owing to climate, soil,
and productions, slave labor is less profitable in Maryland and Virginia than in the more southern States ;
hence, the greater demand for this labor in the latter
States has, since the cessation of importation, caused
a constant influx of slaves from the former. The
breeders in Maryland and Virginia have, for the most
part, striven in good faith for the total suppression of the
African trade ; while those who originally refused to
enter the Union unless permitted, for at least twenty
years, to import their slaves directly from Africa,
have since evinced very little desire to secure to their
neighbors the monopoly of the market.

Whenever the opponents of abolition find it convenient to refer to the action of the Federal Government
on the subject of slavery, they laud and magnify its
horror of the *African* slave trade, and exultingly
point to the law of Congress, branding it with the penalties of *piracy*. And yet we are inclined to believe
that the conduct of our government in relation to this
very subject, is one of the foulest stains attached to
our national administration. Has the trade been suppressed ? Has the Federal Government in good faith
endeavored to suppress it ? These are important

questions, and we shall endeavor to solve them by an appeal to facts and official documents.

In a debate in Congress in 1819, Mr. Middleton of South Carolina, stated, that in his opinion, 13,000 Africans were annually smuggled into the United States. Mr. Wright, of Virginia, estimated the number at 15,000. The same year, Judge Story, of the Supreme Court of the United States, in a charge to a grand jury, thus expresses himself:—" We have but too many proofs from unquestionable sources, that it (the African trade) is still carried on with all the implacable ferocity and insatiable rapacity of former times. Avarice has grown more subtle in its evasions, and watches and seizes its prey with an appetite quickened rather than suppressed by its guilty vigils. *American citizens* are steeped to their very mouths (I can scarcely use too bold a figure,) in this stream of iniquity."

On the 22d Jan. 1811, the Secretary of the Navy wrote to the commanding naval officer at Charleston, " I hear, not without great concern, that the law prohibiting the importation of slaves, has been violated in *frequent instances*, near St. Mary's, since the gunboats have been withdrawn from that station."

On the 14th March, 1814, the collector of Darien, Georgia, thus wrote to the Secretary of the Treasury: " I am in possession of undoubted information, that African and West India negroes are almost daily illicitly introduced into Georgia, for sale or settlement, or passing through it to the territories of the United States for similar purposes. These facts are notorious, and it is not unusual to see such negroes in the streets of St. Mary's, and such too, recently captured by our vessels of war, and ordered for Savannah, were

illegally bartered by *hundreds* in that city, for this bar-
tering (or *bonding*, as it is called, but in reality *selling*,) actually took place before any decision had passed by the court respecting them. I cannot but again
express to you, sir, that these irregularities, and mock-
ing of the laws by men who understand them, are such
that it requires the immediate interposition of Congress to effect the suppression of this traffic ; for as
things are, should a faithful officer of the Government
apprehend such negroes, to avoid the penalties imposed by the laws, *the proprietors disclaim them, and
some agent of the Executive demands a delivery of the
same to him, who may employ them as he pleases, or effect
a sale by way of bond for the restoration of the negroes
when legally called on so to do, which bond is understood to be forfeited, as the amount of the bond is so much
less than the value of the property.* After much fatigue,
peril, and expense, *eighty-eight* Africans are seized
and brought to the surveyor to Darien ; they are demanded by the Governor's agent. Notwithstanding
the knowledge which his excellency had that these
very Africans were some weeks within six miles of his
excellency's residence, there was no effort, no stir
made by him, his agents or subordinate state officers,
to carry the laws into execution ; but no sooner than
it was understood that a seizure had been effected by
an officer of the United States, a demand is made for
them ; and it is not difficult to perceive, that the very
aggressors may, by a forfeiture of the *mock bond*, be
again placed in possession of the smuggled property."
    In 1817, General David B. Mitchell, Governor of
Georgia, resigned the Executive chair, and accepted
the appointment, under the Federal Government, of

Indian Agent at the Creek Agency. He was afterwards charged with being concerned, in the winter of
1817 and 1818, in the illegal importation of Africans.
The documents in support of the charge, and those
also which he offered to disprove it, were placed by
the President in the hands of Mr. Wirt, the Attorney-
General of the United States, who, on the 21st January, 1821, made a report on the same. From this
report, it appears that no less than 94 Africans were
smuggled into Georgia, and carried to Mitchell's
residence. Mr. Wirt concludes his report with the
expression of his conviction, "that Gen. Mitchell is
guilty of having prostituted his power as Agent for
Indian Affairs at the Creek Agency, to the purpose
of aiding and assisting in a conscious breach of the
Act of Congress of 1807, in prohibition of the slave
trade, and this from mercenary motives."*

On the 22d May, 1817, the Collector at Savannah
wrote to the Secretary of the Treasury : "I have just
received information from a source on which I can
implicitly rely, that it has already become the practice to introduce into the State of Georgia across St.
Mary's River, from Amelia Island, E. Florida, Africans who have been carried into the port of Ferdi-
nanda. It is further understood, that the evil will not
be confined altogether to Africans, but will be extended to the worst class of *West India slaves.*"

Captain Morris, of the Navy, informed the Secretary of the Navy, (18th June, 1817)—"Slaves are
smuggled in through the numerous inlets to the westward, where *the people are but too much disposed to
render every·possible assistance.* Several hundred

* Senate Papers, first Session, 17th Cong. No. 93.

slaves are now at Galveston, and persons have gone from New Orleans to purchase them."

On the 17th April, 1818, the Collector at New Orleans wrote to the Secretary of the Treasury—" No efforts of the officers of the Customs alone, can be effectual in preventing the introduction of Africans from the westward : to put a stop to that traffic, a naval force suitable to those waters is indispensable ; and vessels captured with slaves *ought not to be brought into this port, but to some other in the United States, for adjudication.*" We may learn the cause of this significant hint, from a communication made the 9th July, in the same year, to the Secretary, by the Collector at Nova-Iberia. " Last summer I got out State warrants, and had negroes seized to the number of eighteen, which were part of them *stolen out of the custody of the coroner ;* the balance were condemned by the District Judge, and the informers received their part of the nett proceeds from the State Treasurer. Five negroes that were seized about the same time, were tried at Opelousa in May last, by the same judge. He decided that some Spaniards that were supposed to have set up a *sham claim,* stating that the negroes had been *stolen from them on the high seas,* (! !) should have the negroes, and that the *persons who seized them should pay half the costs,* and the State of Louisiana the other. This decision had such an effect as to render it almost impossible for me to obtain any assistance in that part of the country."

The Secretary of the Treasury, in a letter to the Speaker of the House of Representatives, 20th January, 1819, remarked :—" It is understood that proceedings have been instituted under the State authorities which have terminated in the SALE of persons of color illegally imported into the States of Georgia and Louisiana, during the years 1817 and 1818. There is no authentic copy of the acts of the Legislatures of these States upon this subject in this department, but it is understood that in both States, Africans and other persons of color, illegally imported, are directed to be *sold for the benefit of the State.*"*

We have now, we think, proved from high authority, that notwithstanding the legal prohibition of the slave trade, the people, the courts, and the executive authority in the planting States, have afforded facilities for the importation of Africans. It now becomes im-

* In 1835, the New York Journal of Commerce asserted that vessels had been recently fitted out in that port for the African slave trade.

The Boston Express, of 17th December, 1838, thus gives the substance of the statements made by Mr. Elliott Cresson, of the Pennsylvania Colonization Society, in a public address delivered a few days before in Boston :—

" Out of 177 slave ships which arrive at Cuba every year, five-sixths are owned and fitted out from ports in the United States; and the enormous profits accruing from their voyages remitted to this country. One house in New York received lately for its share alone the sum of $250,000. Baltimore is largely interested in this accursed traffic as well as New York—and even Boston, with all her religion and morality, does not disdain to increase her wealth by a participation in so damnable a business. A gentleman of the highest respectability lately informed Mr. Cresson that a sailor in this city told him that he had received several hundred dollars of hush money, to make him keep silent, and when he mentioned the names of his employers, the gentleman says he was actually afraid to repeat them, so high do they stand in society. A captain in the merchant service, from New York, was lately offered his own terms by two different houses, provided he would undertake a slave voyage."

Of the truth of these statements we know nothing.

portant to inquire how far the Federal Government has enforced the penalties imposed by the Act forbidding the trade.

On the 7th January, 1819, Joseph Nourse, Register of the Treasury, in an official document submitted to Congress, certified that there were no records in the Treasury Department of any forfeitures under the Act of 1807, abolishing the slave trade! So that notwithstanding the thirteen or fifteen thousand slaves, said by southern members of Congress to be annually smuggled into the United States — notwithstanding American citizens were declared by a Judge of the Supreme Court to be " steeped to their very mouths in this stream of iniquity," *not one single forfeiture* had in eleven years reached the Treasury of the United States! Mr. Nourse, however, states, that it was *understood* that there had been recently *two* forfeitures, one in South Carolina, and the other in Alabama. Respecting the first, we have no information; of the latter, we are able to present the following extraordinary history.

The Collector at Mobile, writing Nov. 15, 1818, to the Secretary of the Treasury, remarks, " Should West Florida be given up to the Spanish authorities, both the American and Spanish vessels, it is to be apprehended, will be employed in the importation of slaves, with an ultimate destination to this country; and even in its present situation, the greatest facilities are afforded for obtaining slaves from Havana and elsewhere through West Florida. *Three* vessels, it is true, were taken in the attempt last summer, but this was owing rather to *accident* than any well-timed arrangement to prevent the trade."

These three vessels brought in 107 slaves. By
what mistake they were captured we are not informed, but another letter from the Collector shows us
how the "accident" was remedied. "The vessels
and cargoes and slaves have been delivered on *bonds;*
the former to the owners, and the slaves to three other
persons. The Grand Jury found true bills against
the owners of the vessels, masters and supercargo—
all of whom have been discharged—why or wherefore,
I cannot say, except that it could *not* be for want of
proof against them." From this letter it is most probable that the forfeiture of which Mr. Nourse had
heard, if any in fact occurred, was the collusive forfeiture of the Bonds.*

We most freely acknowledge, that so far as the
statute book is to be received as evidence, there can
be no question of the sincerity and zeal with which
the Federal Government has labored to suppress the
African slave trade : but laws do not execute themselves, and we shall now appeal to the statute book,
and to the minutes of Congress, to convict the Government of gross hypocrisy and duplicity.

It is difficult to understand why men who are engaged in breeding slaves for the market, or why men
who are employed in buying and working slaves,
should have any moral or religious scruples about the
African trade ; and when we find political leaders pro-
fessing to be ready to sacrifice the Union to secure
the perpetuity of the *American* trade, we may surely
be excused for doubting the sincerity of their denunciations against the foreign traffic.

* The documents we have quoted on this subject, are to bo
found in Reports of Committees.—1st Ses. 21st Cong. No. 348.

In the year 1817, a new and sudden zeal was excited in Congress for the abolition of the trade, and this zeal, as we shall see, was the offspring of the efforts of Virginia to colonize the free blacks. The legislature of that State had for years been anxious to get rid, not of the slaves, but of the free negroes. On the 1st January, 1817, the Colonization Society, the result of Virginia policy, was organized at Washington, and immediately presented a memorial to Congress, praying for national countenance. The committee to whom this memorial was referred, reported (11th Feb.) two resolutions:—1st, Calling on the President to enter into negotiations with foreign powers for the " entire and immediate abolition of the traffic in slaves ;" and 2d, asking him to obtain the consent of Great Britain to our colonizing free people of color at Sierra Leone. Thus early was the cause of Colonization connected with the agitation in Congress about the slave trade ; a connection from which, as we shall presently see, the Society reaped a very large pecuniary advantage. The resolutions were not acted on, and the next session, Mr. Mercer, regarded in Virginia as the father of the Society, succeeded in getting a vote of the House (Dec. 30th, 1817,) instructing the committee on the memorial from the Society, to report on the expediency of rendering the laws against the slave-trade more effectual. Of this committee Mr. Mercer was himself the chairman ; and he recommended in his report, that the President should take measures for procuring *suitable territory in Africa for colonizing free people of color with their own consent ;* and that armed vessels should occasionally be sent to Africa for the purpose of interrupting the trade. The suggestions of the committee were not adopted, but the ensuing session, (3d March, 1819,) a new act against the slave trade was passed, which gave "a local habitation" to the present colony of Monrovia; and was equivalent to a liberal and national grant to the Society. By this act, the President was authorized to restore to their country, such Africans as might be captured on board of slavers, or illegally introduced into the United States; and he was to appoint agents on the coast to receive them. Mr. Monroe, then President of the United States, was a zealous colonizationist, and was afterwards placed at the head of an auxiliary. Let us see what use he made of the powers entrusted to him by the act of 1819. Many years after, an inquiry was instituted in Congress as to the expenditures under this law, and the Secretary of the Navy (1830,) reported that " 252 persons* of this description (recaptured Africans,) have been removed to the settlement provided by the Colonization Society on the coast of Africa; and that there had been expended therefor, the sum of *two hundred and sixty-four thousand seven hundred and*

* We have not been able to ascertain from what sources these Africans were obtained, but that they were not all of them trophies of the zeal of our cruisers in the cause of humanity, appears from the following extracts from official documents. "There are now in the charge of the Marshal of Georgia, 248 Africans taken out of a South American privateer, the "General Ramirez," *whose crew mutinied, and brought the vessel into St. Mary's, Georgia.*—Letter of Secretary of Navy, 7th February, 1821. "A decision of the Supreme Court, in the case of the 'General Ramirez,' placed under the control of the Government from 125 to 130 Africans, who were brought into Georgia, and arrangements are making *to send them to the Agency.*"—(Liberia.)—Report of Secretary of Navy, Dec. 2d, 1825.

ten dollars. * * * The practice has been to furnish these persons with provisions for a period of time after being landed in Africa, varying from six months to one year; to provide them with houses, arms, and ammunition; to pay for the erection of fortifications, for the building of vessels for their use, and in short to *render all the aid required for the founding and support of a colonial establishment.*"

A report from Amos Kendall, Fourth Auditor of the Treasury, discloses more particularly the manner in which the "*Act in addition to the Acts prohibiting the slave trade,*" was made subservient to the purposes of the Colonization Society.

"In May, 1822, the Secretary of the Navy directed that *ten* liberated Africans should be delivered to Mr. J. Ashmun for transportation to Africa. The Secretary authorized him to take out at the *expense of the Government,* 15,000 hard brick, 5,000 feet of assorted timber, 30 barrels of ship bread, eight of tar, four of pitch, four of rosin, and two of turpentine. * * *

"In the simple grant of power to an agent to *receive* recaptured negroes, it requires broad construction to find a grant of authority to colonize them, to build houses for them, to furnish them with farming utensils, to pay instructers to teach them, to purchase ships for their commerce, to build forts for their protection, to supply them with arms and munitions, and to employ the army and navy in their defence.*"

It cannot be denied that the friends of Colonization had great encouragement to proceed in their warfare against the slave trade. Accordingly, Mr. Mercer, as the chairman of the committee to whom a memo-

* Senate Documents, 2 Sess. 2 Cong.

rial from the Society had been referred, reported
(May 9th, 1820,) a *Bill incorporating the Society*, and
another *making the slave trade piracy;* and likewise
two resolutions—the first requesting the President to
negotiate with foreign powers, " *on the means of
effecting an entire and immediate abolition of the slave
trade ;*" and another requesting him to make such use
of the public armed vessels as may aid the *efforts of
the Colonization Society.* The first resolution was
adopted, and the consideration of the other postponed.
A few days after, (May 15th,) the Act making the
African slave trade piratical, was passed. But laws
do not execute themselves: and if any slave trader
has suffered death in the United States as a pirate,
we confess our ignorance of the fact.*

It certainly required some little assurance in the
House of Representatives thus to order a negotiation
with foreign powers for the suppression of the trade,
when the Federal Government had itself been so remiss in its efforts, that both Houses of the British

---

* In 1820, a slave vessel, the Science, fitted out at New York,
and commanded by Adolphe Lacoste, of Charleston, South Carolina, was captured on the coast of Africa, by the United States'
ship Cyane, and Lacoste sent home for trial. The trial took
place in the Circuit Court of the United States, before Judge Story. The evidence was full and unequivocal; Lacoste was convicted, and sentenced to five years' imprisonment, and to the payment of a fine of $3,000. Had the crime been committed a few
months later, the penalty would have been death, under the new
law, declaring the trade piracy. Lacoste received a *full* pardon
from the President; and the reader may thence judge, whether,
had he been convicted as a pirate, his life would have been much
in danger. The reasons assigned for the pardon were youth, previous good character, and an aged mother.—*Niles' Register,
April* 20, 1822.

Parliament had, the year *before*, (July, 1819,) addressed the Prince Regent, praying him to renew "his
beneficent endeavors, more especially with the Governments of France and *the United States of America,*
for the effectual attainment of an object we all profess
to have in view:" and a negotiation had already been
actually commenced with our Government, proposing
to concede "to each other's ships of war, a qualified
right of search, with a power of detaining the vessels
of either State, *with slaves actually on board :** and a
positive refusal to this proposal had already been returned.   There is ño evidence that our Government
ever took a single measure in consequence of this
resolution; and under all the circumstances of the
case, it is not uncharitable to believe, that it was intended to save appearances.

We must now beg the reader's attention to a new
act, in this farce of suppressing the slave trade.

In 1814, our government concluded a war with
Great Britain, and in the treaty of peace, gave its
assent to the following article.   "Whereas the traffic in slaves is irreconcilable with the principles of
humanity and justice ; and whereas His Majesty and
the United States are desirous of continuing their
efforts to promote its entire abolition, it is hereby
agreed, that both the contracting parties shall use
their best endeavors to accomplish so desirable an
object."

On the 29th January, 1823, Mr. Stratford Canning,
the British Minister at Washington, addressed a letter to the Secretary of State, reminding him of this
pledge, and calling on the American Government

* Letter from Lord Castlereagh to Mr. Rush, June 20, 1818,

either to assent to the plan proposed by Great Britain, or to suggest some other efficient one in its place. *After* the reception of this letter, and *before* the return of an answer, the following resolution was passed (28th Feb.) by the House of Representatives, viz.

"Resolved, That the President of the United States be requested to enter upon and prosecute from time to time, such negotiations with the several maritime powers of Europe and America, as he may deem expedient, for the effectual abolition of the African slave trade, *and its ultimate denunciation as piracy, under the laws of nations, by the consent of the civilized world.*"

The British Minister was then informed, in answer to his letter, that the *plan* proposed by the United States was a *mutual* stipulation to annex the penalty of piracy to the offence of participating in the trade, by the citizens and subjects of the two parties. Mr. Canning replied, that "Great Britain desires no other, than that any of her subjects who so far defy the laws, and dishonor the character of their country as to engage in a trade of blood, proscribed not more by the act of the legislature, than by the national feeling, should be detected and brought to justice even by *foreign hands,* and from under the protection of her flag." He, nevertheless, urged a limited concession of the right of search, as the only *practical* cure of the evil; and he communicated the fact, that so late as January, 1822, it was stated officially by the Governor of Sierra Leone, "that the fine rivers of Nunez and Pongas were entirely under the control of renegade European, and *American* slave traders." He then proposed that a mutual right of search should be conceded, to be confined to a fixed number of cruisers on each side; to be restricted to certain parts of the ocean; and that to prevent abuses, these cruisers should act under regulations prepared by mutual consent; and moreover, that this concession should be made only for a short time, that if found inconvenient in practice, it might be discontinued.*

But the Republic stood on its dignity, and would not condescend to yield a concession which Great Britain, France, Spain, Portugal, the Netherlands, Denmark, Sweden, Tuscany, the Hans Towns, Naples, and Sardinia, have thought it no degradation to make in the cause of humanity.

But still the American Government was *very* anxious that every man of every nation, who engaged in the traffic of slaves on the coast of Africa, (not in the District of Columbia,) should be hung by the neck till he was dead; and forthwith, in obedience to the resolution of 28th February, despatches were forwarded to the Cabinets of France, Spain, Portugal, Russia, the Netherlands, Buenos Ayres, and Colombia, announcing the desire of the United States to declare the trade piracy, by the common consent of nations.

It is generally understood, that a pirate is an enemy to the human race, and may be put to death by any government in whose hands he may chance to fall. If this was not the purport of the proposition to the House of Representatives, that, the trade should be denounced " as PIRACY under the laws of nations, by

---

* Letter from Mr. Stratford Canning, to the Secretary of State 18th April, 1823.

the *consent of the civilized world*," we may well ask, what did it mean ?

On the 24th June, 1823, instructions were forwarded to our Minister in England, authorizing him to conclude a treaty with Great Britain on the subject of the slave trade, on certain conditions. " The *draft* of a convention," says the Secretary of State, " is herewith enclosed, which, IF the British Government should agree to treat upon this subject, on the basis of a *legislative* prohibition of the slave trade by both parties under the penalties of PIRACY, you are authorised to propose and conclude."

Now, it should be remembered, that at this time the trade was not piratical by the British laws, and the English Ministry could not make it so by treaty. We therefore proposed a *condition* with which possibly, they might not have it in their power to comply. The ministry, however, when made acquainted with the condition, felt confident of the acquiescence of Parliament. " The British Plenipotentiaries," says Mr. Rush, in his letter to the Secretary of State, " gave their unhesitating consent to the principle of denouncing the traffic as piracy, *provided* we could arrive at a common mind on all the other parts of the plan proposed."

The treaty, nearly verbatim with the draft sent from Washington, was signed at London on the 13th March, 1824 ; and a few days afterwards, according to a previous understanding, and in fulfilment of the *condition* exacted by us, Parliament passed an Act, declaring that all British subjects found guilty of slave trading, " shall suffer death without benefit of clergy, and loss of lands, goods and chattels, as PI-

11

RATES, felons and robbers upon the seas, ought to suffer."

This treaty provided, in substance, that the cruisers of either party on the coast of Africa, *America*, and the West Indies, may seize slaves under the flag of the other, and send them *home* to the country to which they belonged, where they should be proceeded against as pirates. So that in fact, the whole concession made by us to Great Britain, amounted to no more than permitting her to arrest *our* pirates, and to deliver them to *our* courts for trial; and in return, she granted us precisely the same right with respect to her pirates.

The treaty was submitted of course to the Senate for ratification, which, under the circumstances of the case, one would think, must have followed as a matter of course. The Senate, however, thought otherwise. The treaty was laid before them on the 30th of April; but as they delayed to act upon it, the British Minister at Washington became uneasy, and on the 16th of May, addressed a letter to the Secretary of State, complaining of the postponement of the ratification, especially as the project of the convention had *originated* with the the United States; and as Great Britain " had not hesitated an instant to comply with the preliminary act desired by the President," the legislative prohibition of the slave trade under the penalties of piracy.

The President naturally feeling his own good faith compromised by the hesitation of the Senate, now sent them a confidential message, urging the ratification of the treaty. He remarked that the rejection of the treaty would subject the Executive, Congress,

and the Nation, " to the charge of *insincerity* respecting the great result of the final suppression of the
slave trade. To invite all nations with the statute of
piracy in our hands, to adopt its principles as the
law of nations, and yet to deny to all the common
rights of search for the pirate, whom it would be impossible to detect without entering and searching the
vessel, would expose us not simply to the charge of
inconsistency."

The Senate, after long debates, finally ratified the
treaty, in a mutilated form. They struck out the
word, " America," in the clause authorising the seizure of slavers on " the coasts of Africa, America,
and the West Indies." They also expunged the articles applying the provision of the treaty, to vessels
chartered, as well as owned by the citizens or subjects of
either party; and to the citizens or subjects of either
party carrying on the trade under *foreign flags ;* and
they added an article authorising either party to terminate the treaty at any time, on giving six months' notice.

It will have been observed from the documents we
have quoted, that the slaves imported into the United
States, have been chiefly introduced through the Spanish possessions on our southern frontiers; slavers
direct from Africa, rarely having the hardihood to
enter our ports, and discharge the cargoes; while
small vessels from the West Indies, have occasionally
found their way into the southern waters. Of course
the treaty as altered by the Senate, would afford but
little interruption to this mode of stocking the plantations of Louisiana and the neighboring States.

As *chartered* vessels were excepted, our traders
would only have to hire slavers instead of owning

them, to be exempted from the hazard of being arrested and sent home for trial, by British officers; or
even if on board their own vessels, by running up a
foreign flag, they would escape the penalties of
piracy.

The British Cabinet refused to agree to the treaty
thus despoiled of all its efficiency; but with wonderful simplicity, they proposed to restrict the right of
search on the coast of America, to the coast of the
southern States. This proposition was of course,
promptly rejected by our Minister in England.

The British Government, vainly cherishing the
hope, that the United States might still consent to
some combined effort to destroy a trade they professed to abhor, offered through their Minister at Washington, to consent to a treaty, word for word the
same as the one the Senate had ratified, with the
single exception of restoring the word, "America."
To this, Mr. Clay, then Secretary of State, replied,
that "from the views entertained by the Senate, it
would seem unnecessary and inexpedient any longer
to continue the negotiation respecting the slave convention, with any hope that it can assume a form
satisfactory to both parties. That a similar convention had been formed with Colombia, on the 10th
December, 1824, excepting that the *coast of America
was excepted from its operation ;* and yet, notwithstanding this conciliatory feature, the Senate *had by a
large majority refused to ratify it.*"*

Negotiations have since been renewed on this sub-

* The documents quoted on this subject, may be found in State
Papers, 1st Sess. 19 Cong. vol. 1. And in Reports of Committees,
1st Sess. 21 Cong. vol. 3, No. 348.

ject ; and France has united with Great Britain, in urging the Cabinet at Washington to co-operate with them in putting an end to the African slave trade. The correspondence has not been made public, but we learn from the Edinburgh Review, for July, 1836, that the final answer of the American Government is, that " *under no condition, in no form, and with no restriction, will the United States enter into any convention, or treaty, or combined efforts of any sort or kind with other nations, for the suppression of this trade.*"

To our readers we leave the task of making their own comments on this history of duplicity and hypocrisy ; and proceed to other details.

On the 2nd November, 1825, the Colombian Minister at Washington, in the name of his Government, invited the United States to send delegates to a Congress of the South American Republics, to be held at Panama. In enumerating the topics to be discussed in the proposed Congress, he remarked : " The consideration of means to be adopted for the entire abolition of the African slave trade, is a subject sacred to humanity, and interesting to the policy of the American States. To effect it, their energetic, general, and uniform co-operation is desirable. *At the proposition of the United States*, Colombia made a convention with them on this subject, which *has not been ratified by the Government of the United States.* Would that America, which does not think politic what is unjust, contribute in union, and with common consent, to the good of Africa !"

This document was submitted to the Senate, and on the 16th January, 1826, a committee of the Senate made a report in relation to it, in which they observe :

11*

" The United States have not certainly the right, and ought never to feel the inclination to dictate to others who may differ with them on this subject," (the slave trade,) " nor do the committee see the expediency of *insulting other States by ascending the moral chair*, and proclaiming from thence mere abstract principles, of the rectitude of which each nation enjoys the perfect right of deciding for itself."

The remarks made on this occasion by Mr. White, a Senator from Tennessee, are worthy of observation. " In these new States (the South American Republics,) some of them have put it down in their fundamental law, ' that whoever owns a slave shall cease to be a citizen.' Is it then fit that the United States should disturb the quiet of the *southern and western States* upon any subject connected with slavery ? I think not. Can it be the desire of any prominent politician in the United States, to divide us into parties upon the subject of slavery ? I hope not. Let us then cease to talk about slavery in this House ; let us cease to negotiate upon any subject connected with it."

We have seen most abundantly, that slaveholders have no objection to talk about slavery in Congress, or to negotiate about it with foreign nations, when the object is to guard their beloved institution from danger. It is only on the abominations of the system, and the means of removing it, that every tongue must be mute, and the Federal Government passive. As that government refuses to enter into any combined efforts for the suppression of this trade, and makes none of its own, we may reasonably suppose that our citizens are *now* largely engaged in it. Let us see, if this supposition accords with facts.

PRESENT PARTICIPATION OF CITIZENS OF THE UNITED STATES IN THE AFRICAN SLAVE TRADE.

In pursuance of a treaty with Spain, certain commissioners are appointed by Great Britain to reside at Havana. On the 25th October, 1836, these commissioners wrote to their government—" To our astonishment and regret, we have ascertained that the Anaconda and Viper, the one on the 6th, and the other on the 10th, current, cleared out and sailed from here for the Cape de Verd Islands under the AMERICAN flag. These two vessels *arrived* at the Havana, fitted in every particular for the slave trade, and took on board a cargo which would alone have condemned as a slaver any vessel belonging to the nations that are parties to the equipment article." They remark that the declaration of the American President *not to make the United States a party to any convention on the subject of the slave trade,* " has been the means of inducing American citizens to build and fit in their ports vessels only calculated for piracy, or the slave trade— to enter this port, and in concert with the Havana slave traders, to take on board a prohibited cargo *manacles* &c., and proceed openly to that notorious depot for this iniquitous traffic, the Cape de Verd Island, *under shelter of the national flag;* and we may add, that while these AMERICAN SLAVERS were making their final arrangements for departure, the Havana was *visited more than once by American ships of war.*" This statement and others we are about to present to the reader, explain *the practical results and probably the secret motives* of the rejection by the Senate of the slave trade convention with Great Britain. The

commissioners proceed:—" Two AMERICAN vessels, the
Fanny Butler and Rosanna, have proceeded to the
Cape de Verd Islands and the coast of Africa under
the AMERICAN flag, upon the same inhuman speculation. . . . We cannot conceal our deep regret at the
NEW and DREADFUL impetus imparted to the slave
trade of this island, by the manner in which some
American citizens impunibly violate every law, by
embarking *openly* for the coast of Africa under their
NATIONAL flag, with the *avowed* purpose of bringing
slaves to this market. We are likewise assured, that
it is intended by means of this *flag* to supply slaves
for the vast province of TEXAS. Agents from there,
being in constant communication with the Havana
Slave Merchants."*

We are fearful of trespassing upon the patience of
the reader, while we enter into the details necessary
to demonstrate the increased activity given to the
trade by the action of the Federal Government ; but
these details are essential to an exhibition of the horrible duplicity of the government, and the foul disgrace in which the flag of the Republic is steeped,
by being made the ægis of the very wretches whom
our legislators pretend to regard as pirates.

We learn from Buxton's late work on the present state of the trade, that

" The Venus, said to be the sharpest clipper built
vessel ever constructed at Baltimore, left that place
in July, 1838, and arrived at Havana on the 4th
August, following. She sailed from thence in September for Mozambique ; there she took a cargo of
slaves, being all this time under *the flag of the United*

* Buxton's African Slave Trade, p. 21.

States. On the 7th of January, 1839, she landed 860 negroes near Havana under Portuguese *colors,*" p. 23.

In certain documents, lately published by the British Parliament we have the *names* of *eleven* vessels, which sailed under the flag of the United States, from Havana to Africa for slaves in 1837, and of *nineteen* more, which sailed in 1838. Major McGregor, special magistrate for the Bahamas, in a letter to Mr. Buxton mentions the wreck of the schooner Invincible, a slaver, on the 28th October, 1837, and adds,

" The captain's name was Potts, a native of Florida. The vessel was fitted out at Baltimore in America, and three fourths of the crew were natives of the United States, although they pretended to be only passengers."

The Major also mentions another slaver, with a cargo of 160 Africans, being wrecked on one of the Islands, and says,

" This pretended Portuguese vessel was fitted out at Baltimore, United States, having been formerly a Pilot boat, called the Washington. The supercargo was an American citizen of Baltimore." p. 23. 186.

Mr. Mitchel Thompson, an officer on board the British ship of war Sappho, thus wrote at Jamaica in the spring of 1839, to a gentleman of Philadelphia.

" Almost *half* the vessels employed in this trade and furnished to either the Spaniards or the Portuguese are from America, and seem to have been built at Baltimore, from which place they sail chartered for some port in Cuba with *lumber ;* which lumber is converted into slave decks on their arrival at the destined port. To this is now added copper, casks, and food, with the necessary slave irons ; and now also is added the requisite number of Spaniards as part complement of the ship's company ; *with American papers and flag, they escape our cruisers, as the concession of the right of mutual search has not been made by America.*"

A recent letter from an officer of the British ship of war Pelican, published in the London papers, mentions that this ship had lately captured an AMERICAN schooner, the Octavia of Baltimore with 220 slaves.

The Editor of the Baltimore Chronicle states, that Captain McDonald of the brig North, just arrived from Africa, reported that the Captain of the British brig of war Partaga, told him in conversation, that they had fallen in with several vessels which had the appearance of being slavers, but having *American colors and papers* furnished by the Consul at Havana, he had to let them pass ; but afterwards he fell in with them with *slaves on board*, that being proof positive of their true character.

Mr. Buchanan, Governor of Liberia, in a letter written from the Colony and published in the New York Journal of Commerce of July 6, 1839, says,

" Never was the AMERICAN FLAG so extensively used by those pirates upon liberty and humanity as present. Probably THREE FOURTHS of the vessels boarded by the English cruisers and found to be slavers are PROTECTED by American PAPERS AND THE AMERICAN FLAG."*

* The American and Russian flag, bear very different relations towards the African slave trade. On the 2d April, 1836, the Russian Consul in New York, published in the papers, by special instructions from his Government, a " Consular Notice," in which he declared that " no slave trader, in any circumstances whatever, when seized under the *Russian flag*, or otherwise, can invoke the aid of the Imperial Government to screen him from just and well merited punishment."

In the spring of 1839, three American slavers were captured by British cruisers and carried into Sierra Leone. They were the Clara, Wyoming, and Eagle, all under AMERICAN captains and furnished with AMERICAN papers. They had no slaves on board, but were fitted up for the trade, having slave decks, manacles, &c. &c.

At Sierra Leone it was decided that the English courts had no jurisdiction over these vessels, and of course that their capture was unauthorized. But inasmuch as the character of the vessels was obvious, and they were engaged in a trade declared piratical by the American Congress, it was deemed both prudent and friendly to send them home for trial, and they arrived at New-York in June last, under the charge of a British ship of war. A more unwelcome present could not have been offered to the Federal Government than these three slavers. An acceptance of them would have involved various inconvenient consequences. In the first place the President would have been compelled by a due regard to the feelings of his southern constituents to inquire by what authority British officers had presumed to arrest these ships, interrupt their voyages, and transport them across the Atlantic; contrary to the known and recorded will of the Senate of the United States? This would have led to an embarrassing negotiation, and likewise to a very undesirable discussion in the newspapers, and would probably have strengthened the hostility at the North to slavery and the slave trade. If, on the other hand, the government acquiesced in this treatment of American slavers, then our courts would be occupied in trials in which it would be im-

possible to avoid touching upon "the delicate subject," and men might be sentenced to the gallows,
merely for buying and selling their fellow-men. It
would moreover be permitting Great Britain to do
without a treaty what she had entreated us to permit
her to do by treaty, and which we had refused. An
expedient was adopted which avoided these embarrassments. The Government, it is said, thought proper not to recognize these ships as American property, and therefore declined receiving them. By this
course all public judicial investigations and disclosures were prevented ; and the whole matter hushed
up as quickly as possible. The avowed reasons for
this decision have not been made public.

We will now recall to the recollection of our readers the remark of the British commissioners, that
"while the American slavers were making their final
arrangements for departure, the Havana was visited
more than once by American ships of war." In other
words our naval officers showed no disposition to arrest such of their countrymen as were engaged in the
slave trade, and to send them home for trial and punishment. It no doubt seems very strange to foreigners that the American navy should be so exceedingly
remiss in seconding the zeal of the Federal Government in suppressing the slave trade—but it is a trite
remark that foreigners cannot understand our institutions—the conduct of the navy is perfectly natural,
and precisely such as might rationally be expected.
We have no knowledge of any slaver having been mo-
lested by an American armed vessel for the last fifteen years. It is not necessary for our cruisers to go
to Africa to capture slavers. The trade passes our

very doors, and slavers are to be found by *those who look for them* off the port of Baltimore, and along the shores of Cuba and Texas.

The New York Journal of Commerce, speaking of the seizure of slavers by *British* cruisers remarks, "The capture of a slaver by an *American* cruiser is a thing unheard of for many years, and wholly unexpected. Scores of slave vessels are caught every year by British cruisers, and we will not do our national vessels the injustice to suppose that they never could catch any, if they were so *disposed.*"

But why should they be "so disposed?" About one half of our naval officers are the sons of slaveholders, and can we expect that they will voluntarily assist in bringing men to the gibbet for trading in African savages, while their own fathers are engaged in buying and selling their fellow-countrymen?

Again, pecuniary reward, professional promotion, and public applause, are the chief incentives to military enterprise. Our officers have been recently taught, that efforts to capture or destroy *fugitive slaves* will be liberally rewarded from the national treasury; but when have they been *paid* for capturing slaves?

It is natural that our young and ardent officers should pant for promotion, and that they should turn their anxious and expectant gaze upon the dispenser of professional favors, the SECRETARY OF THE NAVY. Should they read this gentleman's work, "Slavery in the United States," they will have little hope of getting into his good graces by any exhibition of zeal against the African slave trade. They will learn from the head of the naval department, that the introduction of negro slaves into our country was in "accord-

12

ance with the sanction of Holy writ, as conveyed in
the twenty-fifth chapter of Leviticus," p. 42—and
they will be led to infer the benevolent tendency of
the traffic from the following authoritative declaration
of the innocency and happiness of slavery itself.

"That slavery is a great moral evil, or that its existence or continuance detracts one tittle, one *atom*
from the happiness of the slaves, our own experience
and observation directly contradict." p. 126.

We presume Mr. Paulding alludes to the experience and observation acquired in his intercourse with
coffle-drivers during his excursion in 1816. Our officers are moreover instructed by the Secretary, that
although,

"The white and black races of men are probably
the nearest to each other of all these varieties (ani-
mals with similar instincts) they are not homogeni-
ous any more than the orang-outang, the ape, the ba-
boon, and the monkey, who possibly may ere long find
a new sect of philanthropists to sustain their claim to
amalgamation." p. 271.

But should our officers inquire how far public opinion would justify and commend them for breaking up
the voyages of American merchants, seizing their vessels, and exposing their commanders and crews to an
infamous death, what answer would be returned by
facts?

The Editor of the New York Journal of Commerce
declared, in his paper of 20th June, 1835,

"We pledge ourselves to prove to the satisfaction
of the President, or Secretary of War, that slave ships
have, within the past year, been **actually fitted out at
the port of New York**."

Has the Secretary of War, the President, or any grand jury called on the editor to redeem his pledge?

The New Orleans Courier of 21st May, 1839, after commenting on the present extent of the African slave trade remarks—

"If such have been the results produced by the injudicious efforts of the English philanthropists, we may well doubt the *policy* of the law of Congress which has prohibited the importation of slaves from Africa—a policy, that by all we can learn, has no other effect than to cause the planter of Louisiana to pay to the Virginia slaveholder one thousand dollars for a negro which *now* in Cuba, and by-and-by in Texas, may be bought for half the money. It is known to those acquainted with the character of the African, that he is more patient and less unruly than the Virginia or Maryland negro—his very ignorance of many things, makes him less *dangerous* in a community like ours, and his constitution is better suited to our climate. In transporting him from his own country, his position too in civilization is bettered, not worsted.

"The more we examine and reflect on the policy the TEXANS are likely to pursue in this matter openly or covertly, the more we are convinced that Texas should be annexed to the Union, or else *Congress should repeal the law prohibiting the importation of slaves from Africa.* Otherwise the culture of sugar and cotton in Louisiana will suffer greatly by the cheaper labor which the planters of Cuba and Texas can and will employ."

Here we find a public and cold-blooded proposal to re-open the African slave trade. And was this proposal received with horror by the public? Alas! even the northern press has scarcely condemned it. Multitudes of our papers have not noticed it—others have republished the article without a single remark, and the " New York Express," a leading Whig and commercial journal, introduces the diabolical proposal to its readers as " the following *interesting* comments of the New-Orleans Courier." Openly to approve the proposal might offend some fanatical subscribers— openly to condemn it, might injure the Whig party at the South.

The New York " Courier and Enquirer," another Whig and commercial journal, contained (27th July, 1839,) the following editorial,—

"Rio Janeiro papers have reached us to the 31st May last. The chief information from Brazil, which they contain of *interest here*, is that of the capture of two vessels under Portuguese colors by a British ship of war, shortly after leaving Rio, on suspicion that they were fitted out for the slave trade. We are not astonished that these captures should have excited much indignation at Rio. Whatever may be thought of the trade itself *the people generally are engaged in it and interested in its success*, and it is asking a little too much of them to remain quiet while foreign vessels enter their harbor, take in provisions, remain there as long as it suits their purpose, and then sally forth, break up their enterprises, and bring back their property to be condemned under their very noses."

This appeared shortly after the three American slavers, captured by British cruisers, had been sent into New York—hence the indignation of the editor —hence the news from Rio was " of interest" in New York. It is excessively impudent in the English to take it for granted, that the laws of the United States and Brazil against the trade, were enacted in good faith. It matters not, that Brazil had declared the trade piracy,—and that the cruisers only delivered to the Brazilian government their own pirates. The Brazilian people, like our own, are engaged in the trade and interested in its success, and it is a great outrage for foreigners to interfere!

Let the officers of our navy learn from this, not to break up the enterprises of our merchants, and to bring back their property to be condemned under their very noses.

RENEWED ACTION OF THE FEDERAL GOVERNMENT IN BEHALF OF THE COLONIZATION SOCIETY.

We have already seen the character and extent of the aid afforded by the Government to the Colonization Society under pretence of providing for *recaptured* Africans. Some of the southern members of Congress, not fully understanding the true tendency of this society, and believing its influence hostile to slavery, objected to this aid on constitutional grounds, and it was discontinued, after an expenditure of $264,000. That the society is now more justly estimated appears from the following recent testimonies in its behalf.

On the 10th of January, 1839, Mr. Henry Wise, a member of Congress from Virginia, delivered an address before the Colonization Society of that State. He remarked, that a few years since he became suspicious of the Society in consequence of the sentiments avowed by some of its members. That

12*

he had before that time been " the zealous and active friend and advocate of the great original principles of the design, *to secure and fortify the institution of slavery itself* by colonizing the free people of color ;" but he confesses that " the line of demarcation is *now* too strongly drawn between abolition and colonization ever to be crossed. Their principles are diametrically opposed to each other, and their warfare will tend to press each to occupy its appropriate ground and position. The Colonization Society must now maintain that great original principle upon which it was founded, "*friendship to the slaveholder.*"

In the month previous to the delivery of this speech the Baldwin (Alabama) Colonization Society issued an address recommending colonization,

" Because it proposes to remove from among us a degraded, useless, and vicious race.

" Because we consider the measure of all others best calculated to preserve good order and proper discipline among *our slaves.*

" Therefore we deem the plan of removing them (free blacks) from the United States, the most effectual method of counteracting the abolitionists. It is known that *they* are the most violent opponents which the scheme of colonization has to encounter. *Their penetration has discovered its tendency,* and they denounce it as a scheme originating among slaveholders for the perpetuation of slavery. . . . . .

" Nor should it be forgotten, that it (Africa,) is the natural home of the negro race, and at a safe distance, whence *they can never return to the injury of our slave population.*"—*African Repository for March,* 1839.

Thus we see that the society is now regarded as a friend and ally by both descriptions of slaveholders, the breeders and the planters. It is not to be supposed that Mr. Van Buren is an inattentive observer of the signs of the times. Colonization is just now very popular in Virginia, Georgia, Alabama, Mississippi and Louisiana. Mr. Clay's speech was delivered on the 7th February, and was certainly calculated to propitiate the slaveholders. He is, moreover, President of the Colonization Society, and it would be unwise to suffer him to engross the influence of "the most effectual method of counteracting the abolitionists." On the 19th of February, twelve days after Mr. Clay's speech, the intentions of the government were announced in the following letter, which was widely circulated.

"I ought here to inform you that the government of the United States has come to our aid by furnishing cannon, small arms, both muskets, pistols, swords and rockets, and an abundant supply of ammunition, and two fine boats—also made our governor their agent for *recaptured Africans* (*!*) at a salary of $1500 a year—which is so much money *bestowed on the society ;* and I confidently believe that a ship of war will be sent to *the coast of Africa to suppress the slave trade.* There never was a time when African colonization had so strong claims on the benevolent public. Respectfully yours,

Samuel Wilkinson,
General Agent of the American Col. Soc."

Thus, while Mr. Clay can only make speeches in behalf of the great antidote to abolition, his rival is lavishing upon it the public funds under the palpably false pretence of providing for recaptured Africans. When it is recollected that our navy *recaptures no Africans,* and that if we had any such Africans to restore to their own country, they might be sent to Liberia, in the regular vessels at a trifling expense, it must, we think, be admitted that these appropriations to the Colonization Society, and this addition of $1500 per annum to the salary of their governor, is a fraudulent application of the public money, to promote the interests of slaveholders and the perpetuity of slavery.

There are still many at the north who view the *African* slave trade with abhorrence, and great pains have been taken to impress them with the belief, that the colonization of *American* negroes upon the African coast, is the " ONLY efficient means of suppressing it." Here Mr. Van Buren's bounty to the society is regarded as his contribution to the destruction of this commerce. The New York Journal of Commerce affirms that the late grants " will have an important influence in checking the slave trade."

African negroes, we well know, sell every slave exported from that continent ; we have the testimony of Mr. Madison, that the *white* citizens of the southern States would not have entered the American Union, had they not have been indulged in the African trade for twenty years ; and, even now, many of them are anxious for its restoration. But *American negroes* transported to Africa, will put to the blush the civilization, and Christianity, and chivalry of the south, and will manfully resist the temptation to which multitudes of our own citizens readily yield, of making merchandize of their fellow men! Do we seek to solve this enigma by a reference to the *moral character* of our free negroes? Mr. Clay, the President of the Society, assures us, that they are, " of all descriptions of our population, the most corrupt, depraved and abandoned ;" and Mr. Mercer, a Vice-President, pronounces them " a horde of miserable people—the objects of universal suspicion—subsisting by plunder." So far from the Liberian colony being a restraint on the slave trade, it will become a rendezvous for slavers, and the colonists themselves will be either their victims or factors. We cannot spare room for all the reasons on which this opinion is founded. Let the following *facts* suffice.

" The Liberia Herald mentions the capture of *three* Spanish slavers, by the British brig Curlew, *while lying within the harbor of Monrovia.*"—*African Repository for March*, 1836.

" Boats have been sent from the Spanish slavers into the St. Paul's, *and slaves have been bought in that river.*"—*Letter from the Governor of Liberia, 8th January,* 1836.—*Ap. Rep.*

The St. Paul's penetrates the heart of the colony, and the settlements of Caldwell and Millsburg are on its banks!

" Within a year, FOUR SLAVE FACTORIES have been established almost within sight of the colony. *Captain Nicholson's report to Secretary of the Navy, 8th January,* 1837."

" To-morrow the schooner sails for New Sestos, to take on board a cargo of slaves which I have ready there. I have been obliged to have *one hundred sets*

of shackles made at Cape Mesurada"—(Monrovia)*—
*Intercepted letter of 28th September, 1838, from the cap-
tain of a slaver to his owners at Havana, and published
by British Parliament.*

"On the 15th of February, 1838, arrived at this
port, a vessel under American colors named the MON-
ROVIA, last from Liberia, with a bill of sale and list of
crew from the *collector of that colony.* This vessel
had neither register nor a sea letter. I have ascertained, without doubt, that she is a vessel belonging
to Don Pedro Blanco,† of the Gallinas, has put in
here, directed to his agent, for a fit out for the coast,
and that a cargo of slaves is ready for her. There
is a *black* man on board, for a flag captain—*speaks
English well*—learnt that he is a complete pilot on
board, to all the inlets between Sierra Leone and
Gambia. He *cannot read or write.*

"Don Pedro Blanco's *agent in Liberia* is J. N.
Lewis, commission merchant." *Letter of February
28th, 1838, from British Consul for the Cape De Verd
Islands, to Lord Palmerston.—British Documents.*

INTERCOURSE OF THE GOVERNMENT WITH THE INDIANS MADE SUBSERVIENT TO SLAVERY.

It has been long customary, in every treaty of
peace, after an Indian war, to insert an article for the
surrender of prisoners, "white or black," or of "all
citizens of the United States, white inhabitant or

* This letter is dated at *Little Bassa*, in Liberia, and between
Monrovia and Cape Palmas.

† A notorious slave merchant, connected with a house in Havana.

negroes." It is doubtful whether the southern Indians, in their wars, made any slaves *prisoners,* strictly speaking. Servitude with the Indians is so much lighter than with the planters, that the slaves are ever ready to exchange Christian for heathen masters ; and many of them have embraced the opportunity, afforded by Indian wars, of escaping from the " quarters," and seeking refuge in the wigwam.

In 1802 Congress passed a law, whereby the government assumed the obligation of indemnifying the citizens for all robberies and trespasses they might suffer from the Indians ; and the amount of the indemnification was to be deducted from the annuities or other monies which might be due from the government to the Indians. The treaty stipulation to restore negroes was nugatory in practice, as the Indians felt probably no disposition to execute it. Still the stipulation imposed an obligation, and laid the foundation of *a claim* on the part of the government. These introductory remarks will aid the reader in comprehending the extraordinary and iniquitous transaction we shall now proceed to unfold.

On the 8th January, 1821, a treaty was concluded at Indian Springs, between the United States and the Creek nation. The federal negotiators were D. M. Forney, of North Carolina, and David Meriwether of Georgia. By this treaty the United States purchased certain lands belonging to the Creeks. The consideration for these lands was two-fold, first a certain sum of money, and secondly, the following stipulation in the words of the treaty :—

" And, as *a further consideration* for said cession, the United States do hereby agree to pay the State of *Georgia*, whatever balance may be found due by the Creek nation, to the citizens of that State, whenever the same shall be ascertained in conformity with reference made by the Commissioners of Georgia, and the chiefs, headmen, and warriors of the Creek nation, to be paid in five annual instalments, without interest, *provided* the same shall not exceed the sum of $250,000, the Commissioners of Georgia executing to the Creek nation a full and final relinquishment of all claims of the citizens of Georgia against the Creek nation, for property taken or destroyed PRIOR to the Act of Congress, of one thousand eight hundred and two, regulating the intercourse with the Indian tribes."—*See Treaty, Laws of U. S.*—6 *Vol. p.* 771.

For whatever trespasses the Georgians had suffered from the Creeks *since* 1802, they had been compensated by the Federal Government. An opportunity was now offered for wringing from these poor and ignorant savages, compensation for every alleged injury committed by them from the first settlement of the country up to the year 1802! They were about to sell their lands, and were made to believe that they were answerable for every pig and calf which they or their ancestors had ever stolen from their pale faced neighbors. The Georgians, however, kindly agreed that they would not demand more than $250,000; and the United States most benevolently stipulated, that if the Georgians would give the Creeks a receipt in full, that then, whatever balance should be found due on these claims, should be paid out of the national treasury;—this stipulation being expressly declared to be part of the consideration given for the land.

It is therefore obvious, that $250,000 of the consideration or price of the land was withheld by the United States, wherewith to liquidate "whatever balance," not exceeding that sum, might be found due to the Georgians.   This is certainly one of the most extraordinary treaties in the annals of diplomacy.   The claims to be paid are all undefined, and unlimited as to time, except that no one *can be* of a shorter standing than *twenty years !*   And these ancient and undescribed claims, after laying dormant for twenty years, are now to be paid for by a set of poor half-famished Indians, who can neither read nor write—paid for, too, out of the price which the Federal Government is pleased to allow them for their lands ;—and this compulsory payment, and virtual robbery, is disguised under the form of a treaty, to which the Indians are required to attach their *marks.* Among *ourselves,* contracts and debts cannot ordinarily be enforced after *six* years ; but no statute of limitations is permitted to avail the helpless tenant of the forest.   When claims between white men are to be liquidated by a tribunal, each party is heard in his own behalf ; but in the present case, a commissioner, appointed by the President, heard the allegations of the Georgians only, and awarded them what sums he thought proper, from funds honestly belonging to the Creeks.

The testimony offered by the Georgians has not been published, but we may readily believe it was of a character according with the whole transaction. The award was communicated to Congress,* and we extract from it the following summary of allowance

* State papers, 1 Sess. 20 Cong., H. of R., Vol. vii. Doc. 268.

for SLAVES, alleged to have been killed or stolen by the Creeks, viz.:

In the year 1779,	2 slaves,		$800
1780,	1 "		300
1781,	3 "		1,100
1782,	2 "		750
1784,	2 "		1000
1788,	49 "		17,600
	1 " girl,"		250
	1 " negro woman killed,"		325
1789,	8 slaves,		2,320
	1 " negro boy,"		400
1790—1801,	21 slaves,		7,950
Total,	91 slaves,		$32,795

This statement gives rise to various reflections. We observe, in the first place, that through the agency of the Federal Government, a Georgia slaveholder recovers from the Indians $800, for two slaves who had escaped from him or his ancestors FORTY years before! The enormous valuation of these slaves also deserves notice. It seems, slaves are supposed to have been worth, in 1779, when there was no sugar nor cotton cultivation in Georgia, nor man-market in New Orleans; and at a time when the whole State was overrun with foreign troops, and its cities in possession of the enemy, *four hundred dollars a head* —double the price they commanded after the peace.

From the *dates* of these several claims, we may form some idea of the nature of the testimony by which they were supported. Of eye witnesses, it is scarcely possible there could have been one—of family tradi-

tions, guesses, and assertions, there was, no doubt,
abundance. It must not be supposed the Creeks had
to pay for negroes only. In the Indian wars occur-
ring between 1779 and 1802, the Georgians lost various other chattels, for which compensation was
allowed on the same liberal scale. How the value of
a Georgia calf or pig, forty years before, was ascertained, we are not informed; but probably by the
same process by which it was discovered, that in
1789 a "negro boy" was worth $400. But whatever
was the road traveled by the United States' Commissioners, they arrived at the conclusion, that the
Creeks owed the Georgians for property taken or
destroyed, negroes included, $101,319. This sum
deducted from the $250,000 retained by the Govern-
ment, left a balance of $148,681.

Can the reader doubt for a moment to whom this
balance justly belonged? A certain value was of
course set upon the land purchased of the Creeks; a
portion of that value was paid in money, and as a
"further consideration," the United States assumed
the payment of the Georgia claims to the amount of
$250,000. Had there been no claims, the money
reserved would of course have belonged to the Creeks.
But if the extent of the claims was grossly exaggerated, and the Indians were made to believe they
owed more than double the real amount, can there be
a question, that on every principle of honor and equity,
the balance left belonged to the Creeks? Thus thought
the Creeks, and they accordingly petitioned Congress
for this balance, as due to them in part payment for
their lands;* but Congress thought differently, and
not one cent was ever restored to them.

* State papers, 2 Sess. 20 Cong., Vol. ii. Doc. 80.

The Georgians who had been so lucky as to have ancestors who had lost cows, horses, and negroes in the Indian wars, now cast a wistful eye upon this balance. True it was, their antiquated claims had been settled in a manner agreed to by themselves, and receipts in full had been given; and most extravagant compensation had been awarded to them. But still, here was about $150,000, which most certainly did not belong to the Government—and as to paying it to *Indians*, why that was out of the question; and so they modestly asked for it themselves. Their petition was referred to the Committee on Indian affairs; and on the 7th January, 1834, its chairman, Mr. Gilmer, a representative from *Georgia*, reported in favor of the petitioners. He contended that the claimants were entitled, not merely to the value of the property taken, but *also* to compensation for being deprived of its use. "A careful examination," proceeds the report, "of the merits of the claims, founded on the *increase* of the *female* slaves which were taken and carried away by those Indians, would, it is believed, lead to a similar result. Those who are at all conversant with the considerations which form the criterion by which the value of slave property is estimated, know that a much higher value is set on a *female* slave, in consequence of an anticipation of increase. Therefore, as the claimant whose female slave was taken by those Indians, and carried away, had a *property in expectancy* in the issue of such female slave, principles of common sense and common justice would award to the rightful owner a restitution of such increase, or an equivalent in lieu thereof."*

* Reports of Committees, 1 Sess. 23 Con. Doc. 140.

People at the north may sometimes count their chickens before they are hatched; but it would have been a still more occult operation for Congress to have calculated the market value, in 1834, of the children which *might* have been born of the "negro woman killed" in 1788; and Mr. Gilmer himself admitted that the subject was attended with difficulty. It was not, however, necessary to enter into such abstruse inquiries; all that was wanted was the adoption of some rule which would certainly *absorb the whole balance*, and at the same time give to a transfer to the pockets of the Georgians of money belonging to the Creeks the *appearance* of a payment under the treaty. It was discovered that an allowance of interest at the rate of six per cent. on the several awards, from the *date* of each claim, would answer the purpose. Thus, on the award of $800 for two slaves taken in 1779, *fifty-five* years' interest, or $2,640, would be allowed. In this way the claimants would get the entire balance, and might divide it *pro rata* among them. Mr. Gilmer accordingly reported a bill, allowing the interest; and it is needless to say that it became a law.*

* The claim for interest was early made, and was refused by the President, on the report of the Attorney-General, Mr. Wirt, to whom it had been referred. The report, after showing that the demand for interest was not justified by law or practice, proceeded to insist that it was, moreover, *inequitable*. The following extract places in a strong light the injustice of Gilmer's bill, and the servility of the Northern members who voted for it.

"If the Commissioner, in assessing these damages, has given to the citizens of Georgia strict and stinted measure, there is nothing offensive to equity in their asking for interest: but if he has already given them *vindictive*, and even *double* damages, the addition of interest to *such* damages is not, I think, a demand for which

13*

Having witnessed the justice meted by the Federal Government to the Creek Indians, we request the reader's attention to the treatment experienced by the Seminoles, and to

THE ORIGIN OF THE FLORIDA WAR.

It will be recollected, that in 1816, the slaveholders complained that their fugitive slaves found refuge in Florida, then belonging to the crown of Spain; and that, regardless of the obligations of neutrality, a naval force had been sent by the Government up the river Apalachicola, to destroy a fort containing about 300 negroes, most of whom were slaughtered. This territory was afterwards ceded to the United

equity, of her own accord, would cry aloud. . . . . Has the Commissioner been strict in calling on the Georgia claimants for *proof* of the affirmative fact that the property for which they made their claims was *in being, and within* the Creek nation at the date of the respective treaties? On the contrary, he has, in *every in-stance, presumed this fact in favor of the claimants, without proof.* . . . . As to the standard of value—the epoch, with relation to which the values are to be considered, is from 1783 to 1802; that is, from twenty to forty years ago. The region of country to be regarded with reference to the same subject, is the frontiers of Georgia. In relation to *that country,* and in relation to *that time,* negroes, old and young, men, women and children, are valued at an average of $365 80 ; horses of all ages and descriptions are valued at an average of $87 41 ; and in the same proportion in regard to other articles, which I understand is fixing the property at an average of *double its value* at that time, and in that quarter of the country. If this be so, equity, so far from demanding, would revolt from the proposition of adding interest to such a valuation—it would be usury, not interest—prodigality, not justice."—*Rep. No.* 128, 1 *Sess.* 20 *Cong.*

Yet this usury and prodigality was voted to the Georgia slave-, holders by Northern members, at the expense of the Indians !

States; and for several years past, the Government has been waging a relentless and most disastrous war against its aboriginal inhabitants, with the avowed design of driving them from the Peninsula. It is not our design to write the history of this war, but merely to expose its true origin, and to explain the motives which have led the whites to insist on the expulsion of the Seminoles, and the causes which have induced the latter to offer a resistance unparalleled in savage warfare, for persevering and desperate courage and ferocity.

The sacrifice on our part, of blood, of treasure, and of military honor in this war, is well known to be prodigious. THIRTY MILLIONS of dollars have already, it is said, been expended—our best generals have been baffled, and their laurels withered; and our troops have perished in great numbers, in contests with their savage foe, and by the sickliness of the climate. And yet no rational cause is assigned by the Government for this disastrous war. No reason is given why it is necessary, at all hazards, and at every expense, to drive the Seminoles from Florida. The whites are few in number, have far more land than they can occupy, and certainly do not want the wet and unwholesome everglades possessed by the Indians, and into which, we are told, white men can only penetrate at certain seasons of the year, without exposing their lives to almost certain destruction. But were the Seminoles so *numerous* that it was necessary to remove them, to make room for the whites, or so powerful as to render it unsafe to plant white settlements in Florida? We learn from official reports, that they numbered about 3000 !* Major-General Jessup, the commanding officer of the army, and well acquainted with the existing condition of the Territory, in a letter to the Secretary of War, Feb. 11, 1838, makes the following candid avowal.

" We have committed the error of attempting to remove them (the Seminoles) when their lands were *not* required for agricultural purposes ; when they were *not in the way* of the *white* inhabitants, and when the greater portion of their country was an *unexplored wilderness*, of the interior of which we were as ignorant as of the interior of China. . . . I do not consider the country south of Chickasa Hatchee *worth the medicines* we shall expend in driving the Indians from it." Why, then, all this waste of blood and treasure ? We answer—TO PREVENT FUGITIVE SLAVES FROM FINDING AN ASYLUM AMONG THE INDIANS !

We well know how unwillingly this truth will be received by those among us who contend that the North has nothing to do with slavery ; but we appeal to *facts*—and to facts about which there is and can be no dispute.

Florida borders upon two slave States, Alabama and Georgia, and is not far distant from two others, Mississippi and Louisiana. It is not, therefore, sur-

---

* I herewith enclose for your information, a copy of the general plan of operations which I have adopted for the removal of the Seminoles. I have assumed that the round number of *three thousand* embraces all of every description."— *Wiley Thompson, Jr., Agent, Sept.* 3, 1835. " I consider the population, *including negroes,* not to exceed 3000—of which I should say 1600 ARE FE-MALES."—*Joseph Harris, Disbursing Agent of Florida Indians, Sept.* 29, 1835.

prising that slaves from these States, escaping from their masters, should seek refuge in the huts of the Seminoles. We have already seen that the Federal Government have lately awarded upwards of $5000 to the gallant officers and seamen who destroyed 300 fugitive slaves in Florida, in 1816. The terrible example then made, was not, it seems, effectual; for in 1825, the War Department issued an order on the subject of fugitive slaves among the Seminoles, and the Indian Agent at Tallahassee was directed to take measures to enable the claimants to identify their property for its immediate restoration. "Let the Chiefs distinctly understand," wrote the Agent, agreeably to his instructions, "*that they are not to harbor runaway negroes;* and that they will be required to give up such negroes as are now residing within their limits."*

An Alabama paper, speaking of the war, makes the following confession: "It is the power to entice away and instruct in bush-fighting so many of our slaves, that we would wish to annihilate. *These Seminoles cannot remain in the Peninsula of Florida without threatening the internal safety of the South.*"

In 1834, a petition signed by about one hundred of the inhabitants of Alachua County, Florida, was presented to President Jackson, praying for his interposition against the Seminoles.

"While the lawless and indomitable people (says the petition) continue where they now are, the *owners of* slaves in our territory, and even in the *States contiguous,* cannot for a moment, in any thing like se-

* State papers, 1 Sess. 19 Cong., Vol. iv, Doc. 74, p. 82.

curity, enjoy the possession of this *description of property.* Does a negro become tired of the service of his owner, he has only to flee to the Indian country, where he will find ample safety against pursuit. It is a fact which, if not susceptible of proof, is notwithstanding, and upon good ground, firmly believed, that there is at this time living under the protection of the Seminole Indians, a large number, probably more than one hundred slaves, who have absconded from their masters in the neighboring States and in Florida, since the treaty of Camp Moultrie. Within a few weeks several parties are known to have sought and found shelter in the nation where they continue secure against every effort of their owners to recover them. . . . . . . There are, as it is believed, more than five hundred negroes residing with the Seminole Indians, four fifths of whom are runaways, or descendants of runaways. . . . . It is perfectly obvious that during the existence of such a state of things, the interests of this fertile and promising section of Florida cannot flourish; and we are constrained to repeat, that there is no rational prospect for the better, so long as the *Indians are suffered to remain* in their present location."

The petition concludes with recommending " the immediate and efficient action of the government.*"

In the spring of 1839, a sort of armistice was concluded with the Seminoles. This gave vast offence to the slaveholders, and at a public meeting held at Tallahassee, it was resolved, " That the peninsula of Florida is the last place in the limits of the United States wherein the Indians should be *permitted to*

* 1 Sess., 24 Cong., Doc. 271.

remain." For this assertion, the following among other reasons was assigned.

"*If located in Florida, all the runaway slaves will find refuge and protection with them.*"

The New Orleans Courier of 27th July, 1839, in reference to this same subject remarks, "Every year's delay in subduing the Seminoles, adds to the risk of their being joined by *runaway slaves from the adjacent States*, and increases the danger of *a rising among the serviles.*"

SLAVERY, then, is the key which unlocks the enigma of the Florida war. To break up a refuge for runaway slaves, THIRTY MILLIONS have already been expended; and if necessary, thirty millions more will be expended for the same object.

But it may be said, however satisfactorily the foregoing facts may account for the conduct of the Federal Government, they do not explain the astonishing and peculiar inveteracy manifested by these Seminoles towards the whites. Other tribes have without difficulty been removed to the west of the Mississippi; why then do these Indians alone offer a resistance to a superior power, more determined and more heroic than perhaps any recorded in history? Again does SLAVERY solve the difficulty.

It is very obvious that the Seminoles have been universally *exasperated*. Their extreme hatred to the whites, has unquestionably been owing in part to the gross and wicked frauds which they believe (with too much apparent reason) were practised in the treaty of Paynes Landing, under which they were required to remove from Florida. But the great and prevailing cause of their deep seated hostility, is to be

sought for in a long train of frauds and injuries of
which they have been the victims, on account of their
slaves; and likewise in the dread of *Christian* slavery, entertained by the negroes who belong to, or have
joined the Seminoles.

Of all the hostile chiefs, the most active, persevering, and daring, was the celebrated OSEOLA. It is said
that this man's mother was seized and carried into
Georgia as a slave, under pretence that she was the
daughter of a fugitive negress. If this story, which
has found its way into the public papers, be true, the
wrongs of the mother have been terribly avenged by
the son.

That the reader may understand the narratives we
are about to lay before him, he must bear in mind
that the Seminoles, like their more civilized neighbors, are slaveholders—but unlike them, they exercise their authority in such a manner as to render
their slaves unwilling to leave them. The slaves
are in fact little more than tenants of kind and fami-
liar landlords, and regarded with horror the very idea
of being transferred from their heathen to Christian
masters. But there were many of the whites, who
were exceedingly anxious to make the transfer. The
agent, Wiley Thompson, thus wrote to the Secretary
of War: (October 27, 1834.) "There are many
very likely negroes in this nation. Some of the
whites in the adjacent settlements manifest *a restless
desire* to obtain them, and I have no doubt that In-
dian-raised negroes are now in possession of the
whites."

The volume of documents submitted to Congress,
3d June, 1836, and entitled "Seminole hostilities,"

from which we quote, contains many illustrations of the agent's assertion; we can spare room for only a portion of them.

It appears that Conchattimico, a Florida chief, was the possessor of a number of slaves, the title to whom was disputed by another Indian, who sold his *claim* to a white man. The means taken by the purchaser to obtain the slaves, are thus described by the agent in his letter to the War Department, January 20, 1834.

"I was informed by the sub-agent, that Conchattimico sent a runner for him not long since; that he immediately repaired to the old chief's town, where he arrived in the night, and found the Indians and negroes greatly excited and in arms; and that very soon thereafter Vacca Pechassie, with fifteen or more of his warriors in arms arrived, for the purpose of aiding in resistance of a threatened violent attempt to force the slaves out of Conchattimico's possession. Persons interested in the adverse claim, were frequently seen hovering about the reserve; and the chief was informed that attempts had been made to bribe commanders of steamboats, on the river, to aid in accomplishing the capture of the slaves. . . . . . Under such circumstances I could not but approve the order given by the sub-agent to Conchattimico, to *defend his property by force*, should a violent attempt be made to wrest it from him."

Shortly after this, Judge Cameron, of the United States District Court, investigated the white man's claim to these slaves, and pronounced it groundless. Notwithstanding this decision, the claim was again *sold* to a company of whites, who resolved to relieve the chief of his property. But as the chief in-

14

tended to protect it by force of arms, the enterprise was not free from danger. The expedient resorted to by the kidnappers is thus explained in a letter from the late Governor of the Territory to the Secretary of War, 23d May, 1836.

"I herewith transmit you a petition from the Indian chief Conchattimico, to be laid before Congress should you consider that necessary. Taking forcibly the slaves of this chief, after those men had created an alarm among the white inhabitants which resulted in *disarming* the Indians, was an outrage well calculated to rouse them to hostility. The alarm was *concerted* by these violators of all law, solely with the view of obtaining without danger of resistance, the slaves of the chief. I have no expectation the slaves referred to in the petition will ever be obtained, as I take it for granted they have been carried to a great distance and sold."

This Conchattimico was a *friendly* chief, having no intercourse with the hostile Seminoles; but on the report being raised that he was about to join the enemy, *he surrendered his arms* to quiet the apprehensions, real or affected, of his white neighbors. No sooner had he thus rendered himself defenceless, than a party of Georgians carried off his slaves, twenty in number, and valued at $15,000.

We have already seen how profitable it is for a Georgian to lose a slave among the Indians; but Congress has provided no fund to indemnify the Indian master for the slaves of which *he* may be robbed by Georgians.

Another friendly Florida chief, Pechassie, thus complains to the agent (28th July, 1835,) "I am in-

duced to write to you in consequence of the depreda-
tions making, and attempted to be made on my farm,
by a company of men, negro-stealers; some of whom
are from Columbus, (Georgia,) and have connected
themselves with Brown and Douglas. It is reported,
and believed by all the white people around here, that
a large number of them will very shortly come down
here, and attempt to take off Billy, Jim, Rose and her
family, and others (slaves.) . . . . I should like to
have your advice how I should act: I dislike to make
any trouble, or have any difficulty with the white people; but if they will trespass on my premises, and on
my rights, I must defend myself the best way I can . . . .
Please direct me how to act in this matter. Douglas
and his company hired a man, who has *two large trained
dogs for the purpose*, to come down and take Billy.
The man came, but seeing he could do nothing alone,
has gone off somewhere, probably to recruit. He is
from Mobile, and follows for a livelihood catching
runaway negroes with these large dogs."

By a letter from the United States Attorney, we
find that Pechassie was subsequently "robbed of all
the negroes he had, some six in number."

As these robberies were committed on *friendly*
chiefs, and *after* the commencement of the Seminole
war, they excited the attention and alarm of the officers of government, and hence probably it is that official notice was taken of them. They may give us
some idea of the provocations which preceded and
caused the war. Indeed the documents before us in-
cidentally show, that the "likely negroes" of the
Seminoles now in arms, were as strongly coveted by
the whites, as the slaves of the friendly chiefs. By a

treaty made with the Seminoles in 1832, the Federal
Government with its usual solicitude for the interests
of slaveholders, assumed the payment of all claims
on the Indians for "SLAVES and other property" to the
amount of $7,000. A scramble of course ensued for
the money, and a voluminous correspondence took
place between the agent and the Secretary of War,
respecting claims for Indian slaves ; and it appears that
the Seminoles had been harassed for years by the con-
trivances of the whites to rob them of their slaves.
The following is a sample. It seems that a Mrs.
Hanna claimed a negro woman and *her increase*, in
possession of the Seminoles. The claim had been
made known to the war department, and so long ago
as the 8th March, 1828, the following mandate had
been issued to the Indian agent. " The Secretary of
War directs that you *forthwith* deliver to Mary Hanna, widow, or her agent, the slaves *claimed* by her,
and take a bond imposing the obligation on her to
abide by such decision as it may be esteemed proper
to seek, in testing the right of ownership in the property in question." We have here a specimen of the
justice meted by our government to the Indians. A
woman claims a slave in the possession of an Indian.
Without the slightest inquiry into the justice of the
claim, the property is ordered to be wrested *forthwith* from the possessor and delivered to the claimant,
and then, as if in utter mockery, the woman is to give
her bond to abide any decision that may hereafter be
made as to the legality of her claim. Who is to obtain this decision? Certainly not the woman ; and
should the poor ignorant Indian go to law, where
would he look for Mrs. Hanna or her slaves ? From
some cause not explained, the wicked and absurd or-

der of the Secretary was not executed; and on the
2d March, 1835, *seven* years after, a second order
from the Secretary of War directed the agent " to
afford whatever facilities may be in his power, upon
the *claim being established by proper proof before the
competent tribunal*, to have the property restored to
Mrs. Hanna." Should the reader be struck with the
remarkable *moral* difference between these two orders,
the explanation is easy,—the office was filled at the
time of the first order by a slaveholder; at the time
of the second, by a northern gentleman. The agent
now investigated the case, and it was discovered that the father of Mrs. Hanna, about the year
1815, had sold the woman in question, then full
grown, to a Seminole, for forty steers, and had afterwards, as was alleged, *given* the same woman to his
daughter; and on this pretended gift Mrs. Hanna
claimed, not merely the woman, who had now lived
twenty-five years with the Indians, but also all the
children she had borne within that time !

On the 12th of December, 1834, the agent wrote to
the Secretary, that a Seminole woman of the name of
Nelly, inherited from her father " a considerable number of slaves," that a man named Floyd claims the
whole of them by virtue of a bill of sale, and that
Nelly insists that " Floyd imposed on her by present-
ing for her signature a bill of sale for all the negroes,
instead of a written authority to him to recover some
for her."* The agent adds, he has seen no one who
pretends that Floyd paid her for the negroes, and that
the universal impression is, that she was grossly imposed upon.

* A portion of them were claimed by another Indian.

14*

If civilized and Christian slaveholders are ready to murder, or, to use Mr. Preston's phrase, to HANG abolitionists for questioning their moral right to hold property in man ; we may judge what must have been the exasperation of the Seminoles at these multiplied attempts to rob them of their slaves.

There is still another mode in which slavery has operated to produce and continue the war in Florida. Although the expulsion of the Seminoles from the peninsula was devoutly desired by the whites, no inclination was felt to send their "likely negroes" to the west of the Mississippi. Of these negroes some were stolen, others claimed under fraudulent pretexts, and others it was proposed to *purchase* of their masters. General R. K. Call addressed a letter to President Jackson, (22d March, 1835,) asking leave "to purchase ONE HUNDRED AND FIFTY" of the Seminole negroes. "These negroes," he affirms, "are violently opposed to leaving the country. If the Indians are permitted to convert them into SPECIE, one great obstacle in the way of removal may be overcome." The applicant was informed that no permission was necessary—there being no legal prohibition to the Indians selling their slaves. Agents were forthwith dispatched to the nation, to buy up negroes. Mr. W. Thompson, the agent, however, assumed the responsibility of prohibiting these agents from commencing their negotiations ; and assigned his reasons in a very able letter to the Secretary of War (27th April, 1835.) "The intercourse laws," he remarked, "prohibited the purchase of an Indian pony by a member of civilized society, without permission from the agent, and why ? but because the Indian is considered ın a state of pupilagc, and incapable of protecting himself against the arts and wiles of civilized man. If the Indian's interest in a pony is of so much importance in the estimation of the government, as to require such strict guards to be thrown around it, the protection of his interest in his slave should be esteemed more important, by as much as the latter is more valuable than the former species of property. If in the regulation of the sale of ponys the United States exercise a rightful power, the obligation on them to guard the interest of the Indian in his slave, is greatly more imposing. The negroes in the nation dread the idea of being transferred from their present state of ease and comparative liberty, to bondage and hard labor, under overseers, on sugar and cotton plantations.

" They have always had a great influence over the Indians. They live in villages separate, and in many instances remote from their owners, and enjoying equal liberty with their owners, with the single exception that the slave supplies his owner annually from the product of his little field, with corn in proportion to the amount of the crop—in no instance that has come to my knowledge, exceeding ten bushels ; the residue is considered the property of the slave. Many of these slaves have stocks of horses, cows and hogs, with which the Indian owner never assumes a right to intermeddle. I am thus particular on this point, that you may understand the true cause of the *abhorrence* of the negroes, *of every idea of change*. And the indulgence so extended to the slave, will enable you to credit the assertion, that *an Indian would almost as soon sell his child as his slave*, except when under the influence of intoxicating liquors."

We have here a picture of certainly a very extraordinary system of slavery. Slaves abhorring a change, and masters no more thinking of selling a slave than a child! But then these Indians were heathen, and perhaps it was from not adverting to this fact, that General Call took for granted they would be glad to convert men, women, and children into SPECIE. President Jackson was equally inconsiderate. The agent was answered, " The President is of opinion, that the opportunity to SELL their slaves will be an inducement for the Seminoles to remove. . . . Nor is it considered that the permission to the Indians to sell would be an inhuman act. It is not to be presumed the condition of these slaves *would be worse than that of others in the same section of country.*"

To this presumption of executive philanthropy the agent forcibly replied, (June 17th, 1835,) " The remarks in your letter that 'it is not to be presumed the condition of these slaves would be worse than that of others in the same section of country' is true ; yet you will agree with me, that the same remark would be applicable to myself, or any other individual in the United States, as we should, if subjected to slavery, be in the precise condition of our fellow slaves. . . . . Any one at all acquainted with the condition of the negro, as connected with his Indian owner here, could not fail to admit that the change with him would be *oppressively great.*" Mr. Thompson farther remarked to the Secretary of War, " If the department could be satisfied that the undeniable *abhorrence* of the negroes in this nation to the idea of being transferred from the present state of ease and comparative freedom, to sugar and cotton plantations, under the control of *severe task-masters*,* had been made to subserve the views of government, by inducing the negroes to exert their known influence over the Indians, through pledges made to them, accompanied by assurances that their removal west would, more than any thing else, serve to secure the existing relations between them and the Indians, then surely the department instead of classing them with the Indian skins and furs, would require a punctilious redemption of those pledges. I have not heard of a solitary Indian desiring the privilege to sell."

The President at last yielded, and the agent was authorised to prohibit any person entering the nation to buy slaves. But it was too late—the negroes well knew how anxious the whites were to possess them; and they reasonably feared that if the Indians were expelled, instead of being permitted to accompany their kind masters, they would be consigned to the cruel and detested service of Georgia and Alabama planters. Hence, impelled by the most powerful motives which can stimulate the heart and nerve the arm of man, they resisted to the utmost the emigration of their masters, and in the deadly struggle that ensued, evinced their devotion to the Indians, and their abhorrence of the whites by a ferocious and successful courage which may well send a thrill of fearful anticipation throughout the slave region.

* Mr. Thompson was not an abolitionist, but had lately been a representative in Congress from the State of Georgia.

We now submit to our readers whether the facts we have exhibited do not prove beyond all doubt that the blood and treasure expended in the Florida war, have been expended for the *sole purpose of breaking up a refuge for fugitive slaves;* and that the Seminoles have been goaded into their extraordinary and desperate resistance, *by the frauds and robberies of slaveholders?*

THE EFFORTS OF THE FEDERAL GOVERNMENT TO PREVENT THE ABOLITION OF SLAVERY IN THE ISLAND OF CUBA.

At the time of the Congress of Panama, Spain was still at war with her late colonies, and of course they were authorized by every principle of national law, as well as of self-defence, to carry their arms into the dominions of their enemy. Cuba was at a short distance, devoted to the royal cause, and affording a depôt for a naval force ever ready to prey upon the commerce of the republics. Under these circumstances, Mexico and Colombia meditated the invasion and conquest of that island. But these republics, on achieving their own freedom, had given freedom to their slaves; and it was probable that they would manifest equal regard for human rights, were they to become masters of Cuba. These remarks will explain the following extract from the instructions given to the ministers appointed to represent the United States at the Congress.

" It is required by the frank and friendly relations which we most anxiously desire ever to cherish with the new republics, that you should, without reserve, explicitly state that the United States have too much at stake, in the fortunes of Cuba, to allow them to see with indifference a war of invasion prosecuted in a desolating manner, or to see employed, in the purposes of such a war, one race of the inhabitants combatting against another, upon principles and with motives that must inevitably lead, if not to the extermination of one party or the other, to the most shocking excesses. The humanity of the United States in respect to the weaker, and which in such a terrible struggle would probably be the suffering portion, and the duty to defend themselves against the *contagion* of such near and dangerous examples, would constrain them, even at the hazard of losing the friendship of Mexico and Colombia, to employ all the means necessary to their security."*

The obvious meaning of all this, in plain English, divested of its diplomatic circumlocution, is simply that the Federal Government, in order to protect the slavery of the South from the shock it might receive from emancipation in Cuba, would, if necessary, go to war with our sister republics to prevent the invasion of that island.

But so long as Spain refused to acknowledge the independence of her revolted colonies, the war would be continued, Cuba would be exposed to invasion, and the slave States to the " contagion" of emancipation. Hence the cabinet at Washington became exceedingly anxious to act the part of peace-makers. Our Minister at St. Petersburgh was instructed " to endeavor to engage the Russian Government to con-

* Letter of Instructions from Mr. Clay, Secretary of State, to Messrs. Anderson and Sargeant, 8th May, 1826.

tribute its best exertions towards terminating the existing contest between Spain and her colonies. From the vicinity of Cuba to the United States, its valuable commerce, and *the nature of its population*, their government cannot be indifferent to any political change to which that island may be destined."*

Spain also was implored, through the American Minister at Madrid, to be reconciled to her undutiful children. "*It is not for the new republics*," said Mr. Clay, in his letter (27th April, 1825,) to Mr. Everett, " that the President wishes you to urge upon Spain the expediency of concluding the war. If the war should continue between Spain and the new republics, and those islands (Cuba and Porto Rico) should become the object and theatre of it, their fortunes have such a connection with the people of the United States, that they could not be indifferent spectators ; and the possible contingencies of a protracted war *might bring upon the Government of the United States duties and obligations, the performance of which, however painful it should be, they might not be at liberty to decline.*"*

The proposed invasion was abandoned ; but the fears of our Government were not allayed. The war continued, and some contingency arising from it, might give liberty to the tens of thousands in Cuba pining in bonds. A new attempt was made to induce Spain to remove the danger by concluding the war. On the 22d October, 1829, Mr. Van Buren, then Secretary of State, instructed Mr. Van Ness, our minister in Spain, to press upon that court a recon-

* Letter from Mr. Clay to Mr. Middleton, 10th May, 1825.
† Senate Documents, 1st Sess. 19 Cong. Vol. iii.

ciliation with the South American republics. " Considerations," he remarked, " *connected with a certain class of our population, make it the interest of the southern section of the Union,* that no attempt should be made in that island to throw off the yoke of Spanish dependence ; the first effect of which would be *the sudden emancipation of a numerous slave population, whose result could not but be very sensibly felt upon the adjacent shores of the United States.*"

Fortunate is it for the cause of humanity, that the greatest republic upon earth had not the power to prevent " the sudden emancipation of a numerous slave population" in the British West Indies, on the 1st August, 1838 ; " whose result," blessed be God, is and will be " very sensibly felt on the adjacent shores of the United States."*

The subject of the Panama mission was debated at great length in both Houses of Congress, and frequent allusions were made by the speakers to Cuba. Let us hearken to the sentiments expressed by some of our republican legislators.

Mr. RANDOLPH of Virginia : " Cuba possesses an immense negro population. In case those States (Mexico and Colombia) should invade Cuba at all, it

* The following extract from the Raleigh Register, (N. C.) proves that the idea of interference by our Government to prevent West India emancipation, was contemplated by some of the slaveholders.

" *Emancipation of West India Slavery.*

" The news brought by the late arrivals of the determination of Great Britain, to emancipate the slaves of her West India Islands, is replete with interest to the people of this Union. If such a measure is in contemplation, and we see no reason to doubt it, *can our Government look quietly on, and see it consummated ?*"

15

is unquestionable that this invasion will be made with
this principle,—this genius of universal emancipation,
—this sweeping anathema against the white population in front,—and then, sir, *what is the situation of
the southern States ?*"

Mr. JOHNSON of Louisiana : " We know that Colombia and Mexico have long contemplated the independence of that island (Cuba.) The final decision
is now to be made, and the combination of forces and
plan of attack to be formed. What, then, at such a
crisis, becomes the duty of the Government ? Send
your Ministers instantly to this diplomatic assembly,
where the measure is maturing. Advise with them—
remonstrate—MENACE, if necessary, against a step so
dangerous to us, and perhaps fatal to them."

Mr. BERRIEN of Georgia : " The question to be determined is this : With a due regard to the safety of
the southern States, can you suffer these islands
(Cuba and Porto Rico) to pass into the hands of
BUCANIERS, drunk with their new-born liberty ? If
our interests and our safety shall require us to
say to these new republics, Cuba and Porto Rico
must remain as they are, we are free to say it, and
by the blessing of God and the *strength of our arms*,
to enforce the declaration ; and let me say to gentlemen, these high considerations do require it. The
vital interests of the South demand it."

These new republics were stigmatized by this honorable gentleman as bucaniers ; not that they were
robbers, but because they had *ceased* to rob the poor
and helpless ; and the evidence of their being drunk
with liberty, was their *practical* acknowledgment of
the principles of human rights, *professed* in our declaration of independence.

Mr. FLOYD of Virginia : " So far as I can see, in all its bearings, it (the Panama Congress) looks to the conquest of Cuba and Porto Rico ; or, at all events, of tearing them from the Crown of Spain. The interests, if not safety of our own country, would rather require us to interpose to prevent such an event, and I would rather take up arms to prevent than to accelerate such an occurrence."—*Congressional Debates*, 2d vol.

The facts and sentiments we have now exhibited, prove beyond cavil, that this mighty republic volunteered to solicit the aid of foreign monarchs to perpetuate slavery in Cuba, and was strongly disposed to incur the hazard and calamities of war in the cause,—not of liberty, but of bondage.

Having noticed our watchful guardianship over Cuba, we will next advert to

THE HOSTILITY OF THE FEDERAL GOVERNMENT TO HAYTI.

To do justice to this part of our subject, we must beg the patience of the reader while we briefly lay before him a few historical facts.

The Island of St. Domingo was one of the most valuable colonies belonging to the crown of France. It is about 450 miles long, and 150 wide. Its population in 1790, was estimated as follows :

White inhabitants,	42,000
Free colored inhabitants,	44,000
Slaves,	600,000

Total,	686,000

Of the free colored inhabitants, numerically equal

with the whites, many were men of education and
property, landed proprietors, and the holders of slaves.
Still they were debarred from all political privileges
on account of their complexion. At the commencement of the French Revolution, the National Assembly abolished this discrimination on account of color,
and gave the *free* blacks in the colonies, the same
civil rights that were possessed by their white brethren. The pride of the latter led them to refuse submission to this humiliating decree of the mother
country, and a *civil* war between the whites and the
free blacks, ensued. No interference whatever with
the rights of slaveholders as such, had at this time
been attempted, either in France or the colony ; and
the dissensions which convulsed the Island, for a long
time related exclusively to the political condition of
the free colored population. In August, 1791, a partial
insurrection of the slaves occurred, favored by the
quarrels of their masters. In some instances the
free blacks united with the whites, in their efforts to
suppress the insurrection, and in others, they availed
themselves of the aid of the revolted slaves, against
the planters.

In 1792, the French Government sent over three
commissioners, with 6000 troops, to enforce their decree respecting the free blacks, and to restore order.
Many of the planters, however, still resisted, while
others took sides with the Government ; and the dis-
tractions of the Island were now aggravated by a civil
war between the *whites themselves.*

A portion of the planters, abhorring the attempt of
the Government to elevate the free blacks to a political equality with themselves, now intrigued with Great

Britain to seize upon the Island, and thus to save them from the degrading consequences of republican principles. In compliance with their invitation, conveyed through their agent, M. Charmilly, an expedition was fitted out at Jamaica, for the capture of St. Domingo ; and on the 19th September, 1793, arrived at Jeremie. Only a few days before the appearance of the British fleet on the coast, one of the French commissioners, who happened at the moment to be acting alone, in the absence of his colleagues, having received intelligence of the intended invasion, and knowing the disaffection of the planters, issued a hasty proclamation, giving freedom to all the slaves, as the only means of preserving the colony from conquest.*

The free negroes and the manumitted slaves united in defending the Island against the invaders, while an army of 2000 of the white inhabitants, ranged themselves under the British standard. The French commissioners soon after returned to France ; great numbers of the planters emigrated ; and the Island was virtually abandoned to the blacks, except so much of it as was occupied by the British troops. These troops were from time to time reinforced by detachments from Europe and the West Indies—but in vain. The blacks under Toussaint, who was appointed by the government at home, " Governor General of the armies of St. Domingo," continued the contest for about five years, and finally succeeded in driving the English from the Island. Britain being in the mean time at war with France, her naval forces

* The ensuing year, 1794, by a decree of the National Assembly, slavery was formally abolished throughout *all* the French colonies.

15*

prevented all intercourse between the colony and the mother country : and the blacks, thus left to themselves, declared themselves independent on the 1st July, 1798, and organized the Government of HAYTI.

The peace of Ameins afforded Bonaparte an opportunity to attempt the subjugation of the Island, and the reduction of its inhabitants to slavery.

Early in January, 1802, a French army of 20,000 men were landed in St. Domingo, and various reinforcements afterwards followed.

The war was waged with atrocious cruelty on the part of the French, and the blacks, aided by the climate, succeeded in destroying about 40,000 of their enemies in eleven months ; and on the 19th of November, 1802, the wrecks of the invading army surrendered to Dessalines, the black chief. Since this time Hayti has continued an independent nation, perfectly inoffensive in all its foreign relations ; and its entire sovereignty is at present fully acknowledged by both France and England, and undisputed by any power on earth.

It is now important to inquire, what has been the conduct of the United States towards this heroic republic ?

Twelve years after slavery had been abolished by a decree of the French Government ; after the expulsion of the armies of England and France ; when for three years not a hostile foot had pressed the soil of Hayti ; when a regularly organized government was in full operation ; and without one solitary cause of complaint against the new State, the American Congress passed an act, (28th February, 1806,) " to suspend the commercial intercourse between

the United States and certain parts of the Island of
St. Domingo." These certain parts were defined in
the act, to be such parts as were *not* " in the possession and under the acknowledgement of France ;"
and of course included the whole Island. As there
was at this time no war in *fact*, between Hayti and
France, and the latter was prevented by the naval
superiority of England, and her own continental wars,
from sending a single soldier to Hayti ; the sole object of this act, was to distress and harass the Hay-
tians by depriving them of the bread-stuffs and other
necessaries they were accustomed to receive from
this country. It was a piece of wanton cruelty, un-
required by the obligations of neutrality ; and demanded by France in a tone of arrogance, which
would have secured its rejection, had not the intended victims been *black*. Bonaparte, irritated by the
loss of his army, and the defeat of his designs upon
Hayti, resolved to starve, if possible, a people whom
he could not conquer ; and he found in the Federal
Government, a willing instrument of his vengeance.
His Minister at Washington, in a letter to the Secretary of State, demanded an immediate cessation of
the commerce between the citizens of the United
States and " the rebels of St. Domingo—that race of
African slaves, the reproach and the refuse of nature ;"
and he enforced his demand with the information :—
" The Emperor and King, my master, expects from
the dignity and candor of the Government of the
Union, that an end be put to it promptly."* The
letter was written in January ; and in February the

* American State Papers, vol. v. p. 154.

act required was passed, and continued in force for two years.

The invitation to the United States to send ministers to the Congress of Panama, has been already mentioned. In the document conveying the invitation, it was remarked : " On what basis the relations of Hayti, and other parts of our hemisphere that shall hereafter be in like circumstances, are to be placed, is a question simple at first view, but attended with serious difficulties when closely examined. These arise from the different manner of regarding Africans, and from their different rights in Hayti, the United States, and in the American States. This question will be determined at the Isthmus."[*]

The invitation was accepted, and the instructions to our ministers contained the following :—" Under the actual circumstances of Hayti, the President does not think that it would be proper at this time to recognise it as a new State."[†] This, be it remembered, was just a quarter of a century since the Haytiens had declared and maintained their independence, and at a moment when they were enjoying the blessings and exercising the prerogatives of an independent State, and at peace with all the world. And what motive prompted the United States thus to exert its influence to prevent the Congress of Panama from recognising Hayti " as a new State ?"—none other than the apprehension that the admission of a palpable truth, the independence of a black Republic, would prove dangerous to the perpetuity of American slavery. Is this slander ? Let the members of Con-

[*] Senate Documents, 1st Sess. 19 Con. vol. iii.
[†] Letter of Mr. Clay, Secretary of State, 8th May, 1826.

gress speak for themselves. The following sentiments were elicited in the debate on the Panama
mission.

Mr. BERRIEN of Georgia :—" Consistently with our
own safety, can the people of the South *permit* the
intercourse which would result from the establishing
relations of any sort with Hayti ? Is the emancipated slave, his hands *yet* reeking" (thirty-two years
after slavery had been abolished by the French Government) " in the blood of his murdered master, to
be admitted into their ports, to spread the doctrines
of insurrection, and to strengthen and invigorate them,
by exhibiting in his own person an example of successful revolt ? Gentlemen must be sensible—this
cannot be. The great principle of self-preservation
will be arrayed against it. I have been educated in
sentiments of habitual reverence for the Constitution
of the United States : I have been taught to consider
the union of these States as essential to their safety.
The feeling is nowhere more universal or more strong
than among the people of the South. But they have
a *stronger* feeling—need I name it ? Is there any
one who hears and does not understand me ? Let
me implore gentlemen not to call that feeling into
action by this disastrous policy." In plain English,
the slaveholders love slavery more than they do the
Union ; and would sacrifice the last, rather than
acknowledge as free, a people who had once been
slaves."

Mr. BENTON of Missouri :—" The peace of eleven
States in this Union will not permit the fruits of a successful negro insurrection to be exhibited among
them ;—it will not permit the fact to be seen and

told, that for the murder of their masters and mistresses they are to find friends among the white people of the United States."

Mr. HAMILTON of South Carolina :—" It is proper that on this occasion I should speak with candor and without reserve : that I should avow what I believe to be the sentiments of the southern people on this question, and this is, that *Haytien independence is not to be tolerated in any form.* * * * * A people will not stop to discuss the nice metaphysics of a *federative* system, when havoc and destruction menace them in their doors."

Mr. HAYNE of South Carolina :—" With nothing connected with slavery can we consent to treat with other nations ; and least of all ought we to touch the question of the independence of Hayti in conjunction with the revolutionary governments whose own *history* affords an example scarcely less fatal to *our* repose. These governments have proclaimed principles of liberty and equality, and have marched to victory under the banner of universal emancipation. You find men of color at the head of their armies, in the Legislative halls, and in the Executive departments. * * * * Our policy with regard to Hayti is plain ; we NEVER can acknowledge her independence. * * * * Let our Government direct all our Ministers in South America and Mexico, to PROTEST against the independence of Hayti."

Gentlemen when they talk in a passion, rarely talk wisely or consistently. Mr. Hayne insists that we cannot *touch* the question of the independence of Hayti in conjunction with the American Revolutionary governments ; and yet in the next breath, he is for opening negotiations with *all* these governments on this very subject. Almost every slaveholder assures us that the slaves, if emancipated, could not take care of themselves ; and yet Mr. Hayne proclaims the important fact, that the armies of these same governments have " marched to victory" with colored men at their head; and that colored men are found in their Legislative halls, and Executive departments !

Mr. JOHNSON of Louisiana :—" It may be proper to express to the South American States the unalterable opinion entertained here in regard to the intercourse with them. The unadvised recognition of that Island, (Hayti) and the public reception of their Ministers, will nearly sever our diplomatic intercourse, and bring about a separation and alienation injurious to both. I deem it of the highest concern to the political connection of these countries, to *remonstrate* against a measure so justly offensive to us, and to make that remonstrance EFFECTUAL."—*Congressional Debates*, Vol. II.

Thus the gentleman from Louisiana looked upon the recognition of Hayti by other and independent States, as a measure so offensive to us, as to afford us ground for quarrelling with them.

We will now advance twelve years in our history, and see if the lapse of time has softened the hatred of our rulers of Hayti. On the 17th December, 1838, a petition was presented to the House of Representatives, praying for the establishment of the usual international relations with that republic. No sooner was the purport of the petition announced, than vehement objections were made to it, and no less than thirty-two members had the hardihood to vote against even its reception. They were, however, in the minority ; and on a motion being made to refer it to the Committee on Foreign Relations, the Chairman of that committee, himself a slaveholder, advocated the reference, as the best way of stifling the discussion, observing that " several similar memorials had been sent there the last session, which had never been reported on. This would take a similar course ; *it would never be heard of again.*" With this intimation, the petition was referred. A motion was then made to instruct the committee to report on the petition ; but, to stop the discussion, the previous question was moved, and the motion denied by a great majority. A few extracts from the speeches delivered on this occasion may be useful, as showing the temper and logic displayed by the southern members.

Mr. LEGARE of South Carolina :—" It (the petition) originates in a design to revolutionize the South and convulse the Union, and ought therefore to be rejected with reprobation. As sure as you live, sir, if this course is permitted to go on, the sun of this Union will go down—it will go down in BLOOD— and go down to rise no more. I will vote unhesitatingly against nefarious designs like these. They are treason,—yes, sir, I pronounce the authors of such things traitors—traitors not to their country only, but to the WHOLE HUMAN RACE."

Mr. WISE of Virginia :—" We are called to recognise the insurrectionists who rose on their French masters. A large portion of those now in power in this black republic, are slaves who cut their masters' throats. Christophe himself was an insurrectionist and a revolutionist. Their Government has the stamp of such an origin. And will any gentleman tell me now, that slaves, aided by an English army, (and it is consolatory to think, when we are threatened by abolitionists with having our throats cut at the South, that these slaves in St. Domingo, though ten to one in number, never could have succeeded in insurrection but for the aid of the British army,) ought to be recognised by this Government, and that their being such is no argument against it? No, it is the abolition spirit alone which would have us say to these men, whose hands are yet red with their masters' blood : 'You shall be recognised as freemen ; we wish to establish international relations with you.' Never will I—never will my constituents be forced into this. This is the only body of men who have emancipated themselves by butchering their masters. They have long been free, I admit ; yet, if they had been free for *centuries*,—if Time himself should confront me, and shake his hoary locks at my opposition, —I should say to him, I owe more to my constituents —to the quiet of my people—than I owe or can owe to mouldy prescriptions, however ancient."

The consolation enjoyed by this gentleman, from the conviction that the Haytiens are indebted to a British army for their liberty, is not a little ludicrous. There has never been but one British army in Hayti, and that was sent for the purpose, not of emancipation, but of conquest ; and instead of aiding the blacks, it was joined by two thousand of the planters, who looked to it as the means by which they were to recover their authority over their former slaves. Yet this army, thus aided, found itself vanquished by the despised blacks ; and in May, 1798, under **Brigadier**

16

General Maitland, capitulated to Toussaint, the black general. The history of St. Domingo affords much and valuable instruction to slaveholders, but certainly very little *consolation.*

It may not be uninteresting to state a few facts relative to the present condition of a republic which so powerfully excites the apprehensions of southern gentlemen, and to the magnitude of the commerce which our northern politicians are willing to sacrifice for southern votes.

The advocates of slavery are fond of representing the Haytiens as a horde of barbarians. We therefore give the following evidence, published by the British Parliament, and taken before one of its committees.

Evidence of Vice Admiral, the Hon. Charles Fleming, Member of Parliament:—" He could not speak positively of the increase of the Haytien population since 1804, but believed it had *trebled* since that time.* They now feed themselves, and they *export* provisions, which neither the French nor the Spaniards had ever done before. He saw a sugar estate near Cape Haytien, General Boulon's, extremely well cultivated and in beautiful order. A new plantation was forming on the opposite side of the road. Their victuals were very superior to those in Jamaica, consisting chiefly of meat—cattle being very cheap. He saw no marks of destitution any where. The country seemed improving, and trade increasing. The estate he visited near the Cape.was large; it was calculated to make three hundred hogsheads of

* By the census of 1824, the population was stated at 935,000. It is unquestionably upwards of a million at the present time.

sugar. It was as beautifully laid out and as well managed as any estate he had seen in the West Indies. His official correspondence as Admiral with the Haytien Government, made him attribute much efficiency to it, and it bore strong marks of civilization. There was a better police in Hayti than in the new South American States; the communication was more rapid; the roads much better. One had been cut from Port-au-Prince to Cape Haytien that would do honor to any country. A regular port was established. The government is one quite worthy of a civilized people."

In 1831, the imports into France from Hayti exceeded in value the imports from Sweden, Denmark, the Hanseatic Towns, Holland, Austria, Portugal, the French West Indies, or China.—*McCulloch's Dictionary of Commerce*, p. 637.

In ·1833, the imports from Hayti into the United States exceeded in value our imports from Prussia, Sweden and Norway, Denmark and the Danish West Indies, Ireland and Scotland, Holland, Belgium, Dutch West Indies, British West Indies, Spain, Portugal, all Italy, Turkey and the Levant, or any one of the South American republics. And what protection is afforded to this commerce by the Federal Government—a government willing to negotiate in every court of Europe for compensation for shipwrecked or fugitive negroes? " Our trade with Hayti is embarrassed; it is subjected to severe discriminating duties. We are probably the least favored of any people in the ports of the republic. Tonnage duties and vexatious port charges discourage and oppress our commerce there. I am assured that, but for these impediments, the trade from this country with that would be greatly extended. The acknowledged cause of all the embarrassments to that trade is found in the fact, that our Government refuses to recognise the Government of Hayti. We stand aloof, as if they were a lawless tribe of savages. While all other powers have long since acknowledged them as an independent Sovereignty, we refuse to recognise them. Others profit by their commerce at our expense. We have no representative at the island of any grade, nor have they a public officer accredited here. No commercial relation, therefore, exists between the two Governments."—*Speech of Mr. Grennell in the H. of R.*, 18*th December*, 1838.

If the treatment which Hayti has received from the United States, evinces the hatred of our republic to emancipation, we have a proof no less strong of its attachment to slavery, in

THE CONDUCT OF THE FEDERAL GOVERNMENT TOWARDS TEXAS.

In 1829, the Republic of Mexico having achieved her own independence, gave liberty to every slave within her limits. This State had a vast and fertile, but thinly peopled territory, adjacent to Louisiana. In this territory, within a few years past, a large number of adventurers from the United States, had taken up their residence with the consent, and under the jurisdiction of Mexico. These adventurers sighed for the sweets of slavery, which they had enjoyed in their native land; and as the soil was adapted to the cotton cultivation, they became restless under the requirement of the Government, either to till it themselves, or honestly to pay those who tilled it for them. Hence, they conceived the idea of transferring their allegiance from Mexico to another republic less tenacious of human rights. Nor was a large portion of that other republic less anxious to acquire a new market for slaves, and a new territory which would give to the slaveholding interest a preponderance in the national councils. Judge Upshur, in 1829, remarked in the Virginia Convention: "If Texas should be obtained, which he strongly desired, it would raise the price of slaves, and be a great advantage to the slaveholders in that State;" Mr. Doddridge, another member said, "The acquisition of Texas will greatly enhance the value of the property in question."—*Debates*, p. 89. And in 1832, Mr. Gholston declared in the Virginian Legislature, that "he believed the acquisition of Texas would raise the price of slaves fifty per cent. at least." Virginia, it will be recollected, is a *breeding* State, and therefore interested in the opening of a new market. The planting States have no wish to raise the *price* of slaves, but are deeply concerned for the perpetuity of the system. One of their distinguished politicians published a series of essays on the policy of annexing Texas to the United States; a territory, which he contended, was large enough to be divided into NINE SLAVES STATES, which would counterbalance the increasing number of free States at the North.

The Federal Government, every ready to promote the slaveholding interest, commenced a ne-
16*

gotiation for the purchase of Texas, and offered *four millions of dollars*, for the territory.* The offer was promptly rejected, and other means were resorted to.

Texan land companies were formed at the North, for the sale of extensive tracts of land, said to have been obtained by grants, from the Mexican Government. Capitalists, politicians, and demagogues participated in these splended schemes of speculation, and became vociferous in the cause of Texan liberty. At the same time, crowds of emigrants repaired to the territory, many carrying their slaves with them. At last, these men, feeling themselves strong enough, raised the standard of rebellion in September, 1835, and on the 2d of the succeeding March, issued their declaration of independence. The Mexicans, of course, endeavored to quell the insurrection; but, although nominally fighting with their own subjects, they were in fact contending against *an invasion from the United States.* The truth of this assertion will scarcely be questioned: yet it may be well to support it by a few facts. The following extracts from the journals of the day, will, it is presumed, be sufficient.

" *Who will go to Texas ?*—Major J. W. Harvey of Lincolnton, has been authorized by me, with the consent of Major-General Hunt, an agent in the western counties of North Carolina, to receive and enrol volunteer emigrants to Texas; and will conduct such as may wish to emigrate to that Republic,

* See instructions from Mr. Van Buren, Secretary of State, to Mr. Poinsett, Minister to Mexico, August 25, 1829.

about the 1st of October next, at the expense of the
Republic of Texas.

J. P. HENDERSON,
Brig. Gen. of the Texan Army."
North Carolina Paper.

" *Three hundred Men for Texas.*—General Dunlap
of Tennessee, is about to proceed to Texas, with the
above number of men.   The whole corps are now at
Memphis.   Every man is completely armed, the
corps having been originally raised for the Florida
war.   This force, we have no doubt, will be able to
carry every thing before it."—*Vicksburg (Miss.) Register.*

" Since early last winter, a series of transactions
have passed before us in open day, the undisguised
object of which has been to enlist troops, and
procure arms to aid the Texans in their war with
Mexico.   Troops have been enlisted—arms have
been obtained.   Their military parades have been
exhibited in our streets—they have embarked at
our wharf—have proceeded to Texas—united themselves with her troops, and joined with them in war
against Mexico.   Is it not a fact that every stand of
public arms deposited at this place by the State,
have been sent to Texas, with the connivance of
those who had charge of them ?"—*Cincinnati Gazette.*

Meetings were held in various places, and speeches
made, and resolutions passed in favor of the Texan
patriots.

At a meeting in Cincinnati, of the friends of

Texas, it was resolved: "That no law, either human or divine, except such as are formed by tyrants
for their sole benefit, forbids our assisting the Texans ; and such law, if any exists, we do not as Americans choose to obey."

The Federal Government far from taking any efficient measures to arrest this invasion of a friendly
and neighboring State, sent an imposing force under
Gen. Gaines, *into the Mexican territory*, under the pretence of protecting the frontiers !—With what result
is shown by the following article.

From the Pensacola Gazette.

" About the middle of last month, Gen. Gaines
sent an Officer of the United States army into
Texas, to reclaim some deserters. He found them
already enlisted in the Texan service to the number
of *two hundred.* They still wore the uniform of our
army, but refused of course to return. The com-
mander of the Texan army was applied to, to enforce
their return, but his only reply was, that the soldiers might go, but that he had no authority to send
them back. This is a new view of our *Texan relations.*"

The adventurers in Texas had no sooner set up for
themselves, than they adopted a constitution, in
which they aimed,—first, to secure to themselves and
their children for ever, the blessings of slavery ; and
secondly, to acquire the aid and protection of the
United States. The first object was to be attained by
a constitutional prohibition of both private and legislative emancipation ; and by making it a fundamental
law of the Republic, that no free black or mulatto

person should reside within its boundaries ; and the second object, by giving to the United States in perpetuity, a monopoly of the slave market in Texas,— the importation of slaves from any other country being absolutely prohibited, thus promising to realize the golden visions of the Virginia breeders.*

A feverish impatience now pervaded the southern States for the acknowledgment of Texan independence ;—an impatience in which the northern speculators fully participated. Acknowledgment it was seen must precede annexation, since the latter could only be effected by a treaty with Texas as an independent power. Still policy required that this measure should be cautiously managed, lest the North should become alarmed at this scheme for vesting the whole political power of the Union in the hands of

* To aid the deception intended to be practised on these breeders, the President of Texas issued his proclamation 3d April, 1836, declaring that " Whereas the *African* slave trade is equally revolting to the best feelings of our nature and to the benign principles of the Christian religion ; is destructive to national morals and to individual humanity ;" therefore, all officers were commanded to be vigilant in suppressing the *African* slave trade. This precious piece of hypocrisy was worthy of the new Republic. On the 1st of January, 1836, the British Commissioners at Havana, informed their Government, " within the last six week, considerable sums of money have been deposited by American citizens in certain mercantile houses, for the purpose of making additional purchases of negroes for Texas." Buxton, in his late work, says, " I have been informed on high authority that within the last twelve months, (1837-8,) 15,000 negroes were imported from Africa into Texas." p. 25. The sugar planters of Louisiana, as we have seen, are complaining that while they are compelled to import slaves from Virginia at $1000 a head, the Texan planters are importing them direct from Africa at half price.

the slaveholders, and the northern members of Congress be found for once refractory.

Congress met in December, 1836, and on the 22d of the same month, President Jackson sent them a special message in relation .to Texas. He remarked : " Prudence seems to dictate that we should still stand aloof, and maintain our present attitude, if not till Mexico, or one of the great foreign powers shall recognize the independence of the new Government, at least until *the lapse of time, or the course of events shall have proved beyond all cavil or dispute the ability of that country to maintain their separate sovereignty, and to uphold the Government constituted by them.*"

This message dissipated all apprehensions on the part of the friends of freedom, of a speedy acknowledgment, and relieved Congress from the remonstrances and petitions with which their tables would otherwise have been loaded.

It was obvious, however, that if we could con trive to become embroiled in a war with Mexico, we might then seize upon Texas, and hold it by right of conquest, without any violation of our neutral obligations : and that by this process, the annexation might be effected with even more facility than by a compact with Texas as an independent power. Accordingly, about two weeks after the late message, the President sent another to Congress on our grievances against Mexico—grievances about which the people at large knew and cared nothing. This message recommended the passage of a law authorising the President to employ a naval force against Mexico if she refused " to come to an amicable adjustment of the matters in controversy between us, upon another demand thereof, made *from on board one of our vessels of war on the coast of Mexico.*" This proposition was coldly received, neither Congress nor the nation seeming to approve of such a novel and summary way of declaring war; and no one having the slightest desire for war, except those who were anxious for the annexation. It being found that a war could not be had, another game was played. The session was to close on the 3d March. The strongest opposition to Texas was to be apprehended in the Lower House. Four days before the termination of the session, a motion was there made to add a clause to the appropriation bill, making provision for the salary of a diplomatic agent to Texas. There was no time for long speeches, and the motion was adopted with the amendment " to be sent by the President whenever he shall receive satisfactory evidence that Texas is an independent power, and shall see fit to open a diplomatic intercourse with her." The late message proved that the President had not yet received " the satisfactory evidence," and anticipated it only from the action of the great *foreign* powers, or " the lapse of time." Little hesitation, therefore, was felt in leaving the subject under the control of the Executive. The House of Representatives, in which there was a majority of northern members, having been thus managed, and a salary secured for a Minister to Texas; the veil was thrown aside in the Senate, and two days before the end of the session, it was " Resolved, that the State of Texas having established and maintained an independent government, capable of performing those duties, foreign and domestic, which appertain to independent governments, and it appearing that there is no longer any reasonable prospect of the successful termination of the war by Mexico against said State, it is expedient and proper, and in conformity with the laws of nations and the precedents of this Government in like cases, that the independent political existence of said State, be acknowedged by the Government of the United States."

As the whole tenor of this resolution was in direct opposition to the message of the 22d December, and as nothing had occurred since that date to weaken the positions assumed in the message, one of the Senators in opposing the resolution, very naturally alluded to the views entertained by the President. On this, Mr. Walker, a Senator from Mississippi, rose in his place and declared, that " *he had it from the President's own lips; that if he were a Senator, he would vote for this resolution ! !*"

At eleven o'clock of the night of the 3d March, an hour before his term of office expired, and just as the Senate was about adjourning, the President sent them the nomination of a Minister to Texas ! !

The conduct of the Federal Government towards Texas and Hayti, places in a strong light the influence of slavery on our national councils. The latter State has been independent both in name and in fact for thirty-seven years, yet we still refuse to recognise her. Twelve months after Texas declared her independence, she was received by us into the family of nations, and honored by an interchange of diplomatic agents. For thirty-five years, the soil of Hayti has not been trodden by an invader ; only *ten* months before the acknowledgement of Texas, a Mexican army was carrying terror and destruction through its terri-

tory. That army had indeed been defeated, but
another was preparing to renew the contest. Hayti
had long been at peace with all the world. Mexico
claimed Texas as its own, and solemnly avowed its
determination to chastise and suppress the revolt.
Hayti achieved her independence after a long and
arduous struggle with powerful armies, and has a population of a million to maintain it. Texas, when
acknowledged, could appeal only to the fortunate
result of a single battle as evidence of her national
power, while she had no more than 60,000 inhabitants
to contend against the eight millions of Mexico.
With Hayti, we had a large and valuable commerce,
while our commerce with Texas was only in expectan-
cy. Yet has slavery estranged our Government from
the one nation, and led it to welcome to its embrace
another, incomparably inferior in political strength
and moral worth.

The indecent haste with which Texas was acknowledged, and the trickery by which the acknowledgement was effected, were prompted by the desire of
annexation. A southern journal speaks thus frankly
on the subject. " Does any sober observer contend—
can he in the face of facts, that Texas has substan-
tially, according to the usages of nations, accomplished her independence ? Was there not an even
chance, to put the matter on the most favorable footing, that the victory of Jacinto might this campaign
be reversed ? But natural *feeling* has outstripped the
prudence of our Government, usually discreet and
judicious, *and social sympathy* has done what political
precedent, and possibly expediency, might not have
sanctioned. The debate in the British Parliament

17

shows how well *State papers* and official ceremonies"
(viz. the President's Message,) " may delude, or seem
to delude foreign governments. While Lord Palmerston and O'Connel were defending our Government
from any improper haste in acknowledging the independence of Texas, the deed is consummated!"—*The
Port Gibson (Miss.) Southerner.*

The whole slave region, with scarcely an exception,
demanded a union with the new State. " The very
reasons," said the Charleston Mercury, " so intem-
perately urged by the North against it, that it will increase the political weight of the southern States, and
perpetuate and extend the curse of slavery, *are our
best reasons for it.*"

The legislatures of South Carolina, Mississippi, and
Tennessee, all passed resolutions in favor of the annexation. Many individuals at the North had likewise a deep pecuniary interest in the question. They
had speculated largely in Texas lands, but their titles
would be of but little value, so long as they depended
on the faith of the lawless adventurers who possessed
the country.—Could that country be received into the
Union, and subjected to the acts of Congress and the
jurisdiction of the Supreme Court, their purchases
might ensure to themselves or their families, princely
estates. A writer in the Salem Gazette, (Mass.) probably a speculator, in vindicating the annexation, thus
appealed to the avarice of New-England. " It is calculated that the value of one kind of property in the
South, slaves, will be enhanced so much, that that
portion of our country will realize one or two hundred
millions of dollars ; and the South cannot be enrich-
ed without benefiting the North—*the money will naturally come here at last.*"

The people of Texas were no less desirous of annexation than southern slaveholders, or northern speculators. The plan of union was avowed from almost the very commencement of the rebellion. In August, 1836, S. F. Austin, in an address offering himself as a candidate for the Presidency, told the people :—" I am in favor of the annexation, and will do all in my power to effect it with the least possible delay " W. H. Jack, a candidate for the legislature, declared: " I am decidedly and unequivocally in favor of annexing Texas to the United States." Gen. Houston, the Commander-in-chief, intimated that " the annexation was essential to the interests of the new country." The Texan Congress resolved, " that the President of the Republic of Texas be empowered and authorized to despatch a commissioner or commissioners to the United States of America, to obtain a negotiation of our independence, and enter into a treaty with that Government for a union on a footing with the original States." The first condition prescribed for this proposed union, was, " THE FREE AND UNMOLESTED AUTHORITY OVER THEIR SLAVE POPULATION !"

On the 4th August, 1837, the negotiation was opened by the Texan Minister at Washington, by a proposition " to unite the two people under one and the same government." The acceptance of this proposition would of course have been equivalent to a declaration of war against Mexico : a responsibility which Mr. Van Buren did not see fit to assume, especially in the recess of Congress. He declined entering into the negotiation, on the grounds that the United States were at present at peace with Mexico, and that that power

had not acknowledged the independence of Texas.
As this answer merely *postponed* the annexation on
account of an obstacle easily removed, it was entirely
satisfactory to the South; and the more so as the
President's message to Congress on the 4th of the
ensuing December, wore a very belligerent aspect towards Mexico.

This formal attempt at annexation roused the fears
of the North, and innumerable remonstrances against
the measure were presented to Congress.   In the
meantime Mexico, by proposing a submission of her
differences with the United States to arbitration, removed all pretence for immediate war.   Under these
circumstances, the southern delegation in Congress
thought it most prudent not to press the annexation.
The Texans, moreover, finding themselves unmolested
by Mexico, who had become involved in war with
France ; and observing the strong hostility manifested towards the measure in the United States, formally
withdrew her application for admission into the Union.
It is folly, however, to suppose that the project of
annexation is abandoned either by the South, or by
Texas ; nor does it need the gift of prophecy to fore-
see that the first favorable opportunity of making war
upon Mexico, will be readily embraced by the Federal Government.   Should such a war be effected, the
dominion of the WHIP may perhaps, be extended from
Maryland to Panama.

It may not be amiss here to compare the conduct
of the Federal Government towards the Texan and the
Canadian rebels.   The first were slaveholders re-es-
tablishing slavery on a soil from which it had been
banished ; and they enjoyed from the first the sym-

pathy of our government, who took care to interpose
no real obstacle to an invasion on their behalf from
the United States: while for the purpose of aiding
them it labored to excite an immediate war with Mexico. The Canadian rebels were professedly fighting
for liberty, and should they succeed, there was no pro-
bability that negro slavery would crown their triumph.
They, like the Texans, looked to us for aid; but the
President, *now* alive to the obligations of neutrality,
and finding the existing laws insufficient to enforce
them, applied to Congress and received additional
powers. Troops were sent to the frontiers, not to
swell by desertion the ranks of the rebels, but in
good faith, forcibly, to prevent American citizens
from aiding the revolt. No attempt was ever made
to punish any of the abettors of the Texan rebels;
but the *judicial* as well as the military power of
the Government was exerted to enforce the duties
of neutrality on the Canadian frontier ; and indictments
and trials and imprisonments, have taught the impressive lesson, that American citizens may not with impunity make war upon a friendly nation, except for
the purpose of trampling upon the rights of man.
" While Mackenzie and Case are lying in a solitary
dungeon, for attempting to liberate Canada, the Texan agent is openly enlisting men at Buffalo, to serve
in an expedition against Mexico."—*Lewiston Telegraph.*

But hear the confession of the official journal of
the administration.

" There is no doubt, we believe, that *vessels of war* of
light draft of water—brigs and schooners—are preparing in the United States for Texas, to be commanded

17*

by *young officers of the American Navy.*"—*Washington Globe.*

Yet not a finger has been raised to prevent these hostile and illegal armaments. The truth is, a war with Mexico is ardently desired by the slaveholders, and the President was for *negotiating on board an armed vessel.* A war with Great Britain, emphatically an anti-slavery nation, is now viewed with horror and dismay by the whole South,* and the Executive has sedulously endeavored to avoid it.

We have now presented numerous instances of the action of the Federal Government in behalf of slavery ; but our task is not completed. We are still to view that Government, which, in the language of the Constitution, was established " to secure the blessings of LIBERTY to ourselves and our posterity ;" assailing the constitutional rights of the citizen, in order to rivet the fetters of the slave ; striving to extinguish the freedom of the press, the freedom of debate, and the right of petition, to perpetuate property in human flesh. These, we are sensible, are strong assertions —we solicit attention to the facts on which they are founded, and first to

THE ATTEMPT OF THE FEDERAL GOVERNMENT TO ESTABLISH A CENSORSHIP OF THE PRESS.

In the summer of 1835, the Anti-slavery Society in New-York, directed their publisher to forward a num-

* A distinguished southern senator, speaking of the importance of preserving our neutrality on the Canada frontier, declared that in his opinion " a war with England would be the heaviest calamity that could befall the country."

ber of their periodical Papers, containing facts and disquisitions on the subject of slavery, to various southern gentlemen of distinction, in the hope of exciting by this means, a spirit of inquiry among persons of influence and character. But it was precisely such a spirit of inquiry, that the advocates of perpetual bondage feared might be fatal to their favorite institution. Hence they affected to believe that the papers sent to the *masters*, were intended to excite the slaves to insurrection, and they succeeded in maddening the populace to fury. A mob broke into the Charleston Post-Office, and seizing a quantity of anti-slavery papers, burned them in the street. This outrage was virtually approved by the City Council ; and at a public meeting, a committee of " gentlemen" was appointed to take charge of the northern mail on its arrival, accompany it to the Post-Office, and see that no papers advocating the rights of man, should be delivered to their owners. The Post-Master informed the head of the department, that under existing circumstances, he had determined to suppress all anti-slavery publications, and asked for instructions for the future. It should here be recollected that of all the political advisers of the President, Mr. Kendall, at this time acting as Post-Master General, was the most odious to the opposite party. He had been appointed during the recess of the Senate, and it was regarded as a matter of course, that on the meeting of that body, in which the opposition had a majority, his nomination would be rejected. The constitution forbade a censorship of the press, and had the people been disposed to delegate so formidable a power, they certainly would not have vested it in the 10,000 deputies of the Post-Master General. The law moreover expressly required every Post-Master to deliver the papers received by him, to the persons to whom they were directed.

Such were the circumstances under which Mr. Kendall returned his famous answer. After stating that not having seen the papers in question, he could not judge of their character, but had been *informed* that they were incendiary, inflammatory and insurrectionary, he added: " By no act or direction of mine, official or private, could I be induced to aid knowingly in giving circulation to papers of this discription, directly or indirectly. We owe an obligation to the laws, but a higher one to the communities in which we live ; and if the former be perverted to destroy the latter, *it is patriotism to disregard them.* Entertaining these views, I cannot sanction and will not condemn the step you have taken." This letter taught the Senate that the new officer was willing to conduct the Post-Office in a manner calculated to protect the " domestic institution" from the assaults of truth and argument, and *his nomination was confirmed.* Mr. Kendall was at the date of his letter, a member of the Cabinet, and it was understood that the novel, extraordinary, and dangerous doctrine of that letter received the sanction of the President.

On the opening of Congress, President Jackson in his message, recommended the " passing of such a law as will prohibit under severe penalties, the *circulation* in the southern States through the mails, of incendiary publications *intended* to instigate the slaves to insurrection." The proposed law, it seems, was not to prohibit the printing of certain papers, **nor** their committal to the mails in the northern States, but only their *circulation* in the slave region. Of course certain persons, Post-Masters, we presume, were to be required, under " heavy penalties," to stop these papers ; and they were necessarily to be judges of the character of the papers, and of the intentions of their writers. From what code of despotism did our very democratic President derive his plan for destroying the efficiency of the PRESS ? By a contemptible quibble, this plan was to evade the constitutional guarantee of the freedom of the press. It was not to interfere with the press—not at all—it was merely to prevent the circulation of its productions ! The press was still to be free to pour forth its arguments against slavery, only " heavy penalties" were to prevent the people from reading them ! The reason moreover assigned for this proposed high-handed act of tyranny, was a most malignant and wilful calumny. It was to prevent the circulation in the southern States of publications *intended* to excite the slaves to insurrection. Such a proposal from the first magistrate of the country to Congress, and following the affair at Charleston, and Mr. Kendall's letter, irresistibly fixes upon the members of the American Anti-slavery Society at New-York, the charge of sending papers into the southern States for the purpose and with the desire of effecting the massacre of their fellow-citizens. If the President really believed that such was the object of the New-York abolitionists, and such the character of their publications, and if he thought it his official duty to bring the subject before Congress, he owed it to himself, to the country, to truth and to justice, to have submitted to Congress the *facts and*

documents, on which he founded his proposed invasion
of the constitutional rights of his fellow-citizens.
But he cautiously avoided specifying a single fact, or
quoting a single sentence in support of his tremendous accusation, or in justification of his most unwarrantable proposition; and when written to by the acting committee of the New-York Society for proof of
his charge against them, he deemed it most prudent
not to return an answer! Surely the burden of proof
rests upon him, who in a solemn official address to
the Legislature, holds up a portion of his fellow-citizens as miscreants engaged in plotting murder and
insurrection : and urges the enaction of a law to
counteract their execrable machinations.

It is often difficult to prove a negative ; but in this
instance, the falsehood of the President's charge is
amply demonstrated by an official document from the
slaveholders themselves. We give this document,
not to exculpate the members of the New-York Society from a calumny which their own characters
abundantly refute, but to show in a strong light the
unprincipled means to which the Federal Government
is capable of resorting to uphold the " peculiar institution" of the South.

A grand jury in Alabama, conceived the bright idea,
that the publication of tracts at the North against
slavery might be arrested by indicting the publishers as
felons, and then demanding them from the Governors
of their respective States as *fugitives* from southern
justice. It was necessary, however, to specify in the
indictment, the precise crime of which they had been
guilty ; a necessity which the President regarded as
not applicable to his message. We may well suppose,

therefore, that the grand jury would endeavor to secure the success of this, their first experiment, by selecting from the various publications alluded to by the President and Mr. Kendall, as sent to the South for the purpose of exciting insurrection, the most insurrectionary, cut-throat passages, they could find. Behold the result.

" State of Alabama, }   Circuit Court, September Tuscaloosa county.   Term, 1335.

The grand jurors,   *   *   *   *   upon their oath present, that Robert G. Williams, *late of said county*, being a wicked, malicious, seditious, and ill-disposed person, and being greatly disaffected to the laws and government of said State, and feloniously, wickedly, maliciously, and seditiously contriving, devising, and intending to produce *conspiracy, insurrection, and rebellion* among the slave population of said State, and to alienate and withdraw the affection, fidelity, and allegiance, of said slaves from their masters and owners, on the tenth day of September, in the year of our Lord one thousand eight hundred and thirty-five, at the county aforesaid, feloniously, wickedly, maliciously, and seditiously did cause to be distributed, circulated, and published, a seditious paper, called " THE EMANCIPATOR," in which paper is published according to the tenor and effect following, that is to say : " *God commands, and all nature cries out, that* MAN *should not be held as property. The system of making* MEN *property, has plunged* 2,250,000 *of our fellow-countrymen into the deepest physical and moral degradation, and they are every moment sinking deeper.*" In open violation of the Act of the General Assembly in

such case made and provided, to the evil and perni-
cious example of all others in like case offending,
and against the peace and dignity of the State of
Alabama."*

In the Senate, the recommendation of the President was referred to a committee, who reported a
Bill prohibiting postmasters from delivering "any
pamphlet, newspaper, handbill, or other printed paper,
or pictorial representation, *touching the subject of slavery*, in any State in which their circulation is prohibited by law." The object of this Bill was, by means
of federal legislation, to build around the slave States
a rampart against the assaults of light and truth. Its
absurdity was equalled only by its wickedness. Not
a newspaper containing a debate in Congress, a report from a committee, a message from the President,
a letter from the West Indies, "touching the subject
of slavery," could be legally delivered from a southern post-office; and thousands of postmasters were
to be employed in opening envelopes, and poring over
their contents, to catch a reference to the "domestic
institution."

By this bill, the Federal Government virtually surrendered to the States, the freedom of the press, and
nullified the guarantee of this inestimable privilege,
given by our fathers in the Constitution to every citizen. This Bill, moreover, prepared the way for the
destruction of civil and religious liberty. If every

---

* Another count was added for distributing "The Emancipator," but without giving any extracts. It is scarcely necessary to
add, that Williams had never been in Alabama. Yet on this indictment, he was demanded of the New York Executive as a fugitive felon, by the Governor of Alabama.

paper touching the subject of slavery might be suppressed, then the same fate might just as constitutionally be awarded to every paper *touching* the conduct of the administration, or the doctrine of the Trinity. It established a censorship of the press on one subject, which might afterwards be extended to others. Yet this bill, absurd and unconstitutional as it was, went through its regular stages with little opposition, till the important question was taken on its engrossment ;—the vote stood eighteen to eighteen. The casting vote was now required from Mr. Van Buren, who, as Vice President, occupied the chair. He gave it for the slaveholders, and received from them, at the ensuing election, sixty-one electoral votes, by means of which he became President of the United States.* On the final question, the bill was rejected, and this attempt to trammel the press for the protection of slavery, defeated. A very different result, however, has attended

THE EFFORT OF THE FEDERAL GOVERNMENT TO NULLIFY THE RIGHT OF PETITION AND THE FREEDOM OF DEBATE.

For thirty years past, petitions have been presented to Congress for the abolition of slavery in the District of Columbia, and the national territories; and, until latterly, were received and treated like other petitions. But having within a few years prodigiously increased in number, and some northern members having shown

* The two senators from New York, Messrs. Wright and Tallmadge, political friends of Mr. Van Buren, supported the bill. It is due to justice to mention, that the bill was finally lost by the votes of several *southern* senators.

18

a disposition to advocate their prayer, a most extraordinary course has been pursued in relation to them. The reason of this course is explained by the following passage from a speech by Mr. Strange, a Senator from North Carolina. " Every agitation of this subject (slavery,) weakens the moral force in our favor ; and breaks down the moral barriers which now serve to protect and secure us. *We have every thing to lose, and nothing to gain by agitation and discussion.*"

The frankness of this confession is as remarkable as its truth is unquestionable ; and it shows us why the advocates of slavery, instead of meeting their opponents in argument, have sought to silence them by brute force and penal enactments.

One of the most unequivocal and undoubted of all constitutional rights is that of petition, and it is moreover, expressly guaranteed by the Constitution. But this right has been most audaciously nullified by both branches of the national legislature. The Senate have not, it is true, avowedly refused to receive anti-slavery petitions, but they have adopted a course which answers the same purpose. The practice for some years past has been to lay the question of reception on the table without deciding it, and the petition not being in fact received, cannot be discussed, nor any measure respecting it taken. This course is no less at variance with the constitutional rights of the petitioners, than it is with those of the members of the Senate. The rights of petition and freedom of debate are both nullities, if the body to which a prayer is addressed, is prohibited from listening to it, and the individual members are prohibited from noticing it. Would it be no violation of the

Constitution were the Senate to order that every petition, " touching the subject of slavery," should be delivered to their doorkeeper, to be committed by him to the flames? And yet in what particular, are the rights of the petitioners more respected by the practice we have mentioned? The petitions are not indeed burned, but they are left in the pockets of those to whom they were entrusted; and not being received, the Senate is supposed to be ignorant of their contents, and of course no member is permitted to discuss their merits, or to propose any measure founded upon them. Let us now turn to what is regarded as the *popular branch*,—the House of Representatives,—intended to be the special guardian of the liberties of the PEOPLE, as the Senate is of the rights of the States.

In May, 1836, a committee reported to the House, a resolution prefaced with this extraordinary avowal : " Whereas it is extremely important and desirable, that the AGITATION on this subject (slavery) should be finally arrested for the purpose of restoring *tranquillity* to the public mind, your committee respectfully recommend the following resolution."

Here then is an acknowledged, unblushing interference by the Federal Government, in behalf of slavery; an avowed interference to arrest that agitation, which we are assured by Mr. Strange, " breaks down the moral barriers," which serve to protect and secure a system of iniquitous cruelty and oppression. To arrest this agitation, the committee did not scruple to recommend a measure, breaking down the constitutional barriers erected to protect and secure the rights and liberties of the people of the United

States. The resolution reported by the committee, was adopted by the House, on the 26th of May, 1836, and is in these words:

" *Resolved,* That all petitions, memorials, resolutions, and propositions relating *in any way, or to any extent* whatever, to the subject of slavery, shall, without being either printed or referred, be laid on the table, and that no farther action whatever shall be had thereon." Ayes 117—Nays 68.

It is worthy of remark, that of the ayes, no less than 62 were from the free States ! The advocates of this resolution, conscious that it could bear discussion as little as slavery itself, caused it to adopted through the operation of the previous question, by a *silent* vote.

We have exhibited the character of slavery and the slave trade at the seat of the Federal Government, and have shown that Congress is the local legislature of the District of Columbia, having "exclusive jurisdiction over it in all cases whatever." Now one of the peculiar atrocities of this resolution is, that it wrests from every member of the House, his constitutional right to *propose* such measures for the government of the District as justice and humanity may require. Slaves might be burned alive in the streets of the Capital ; the slavers might be crowded to suffocation with human victims ; every conceivable cruelty might be practised, and no one member of the local legislature could be permitted to propose even a committee of inquiry, "relating in any way, or to any extent whatever, to the subject of slavery.

The fact that 62 northern members on this occasion arrayed themselves on the side of the slaveholders, affords a melancholy and alarming proof of the corrupting influence which slavery is exerting on the morality and patriotism of the free States.

This foolish and wicked expedient to "restore tranquillity" to the people, by trampling on their rights and gagging their representatives, failed of success. The petitioners at this session were 34,000— at the next the number was swelled to ONE HUNDRED AND TEN THOUSAND! and the gag was renewed. During the session of 1837-8, the number rose to THREE HUNDRED THOUSAND. Early in the last mentioned session, a member from Vermont presented a petition for the abolition of slavery in the District of Columbia, and took the liberty to offer some remarks on the subject of slavery. This attempt to break down "the moral barriers," threw the southern members into great trepidation, and the scene which ensued, illustrates the system of *intimidation*, to which we have already adverted. The member was interrupted by a gentleman from Virginia, calling aloud, and asking his colleagues to retire with him from the hall;—another from Georgia exclaimed, that he hoped the whole southern delegation would do the same ;—a third from South Carolina declared, that all the representatives from that State "had already signed an agreement." The House adjourned, and a southern member invited the gentlemen from the slaveholding States to meet immediately in an adjoining room. The meeting was held, but its proceedings were not made public. The result, however, was manifested in the introduction next morning, of another gag resolution, directing all memorials, petitions and papers touching the abolition of slavery in the national territories. and of the

18*

American slave trade, to be laid on the table, without being printed, read, *debated*, or referred, and that no farther action should be had thereon. Through the acquiescence of northern members, it was passed by a *silent vote*.

At the beginning of the next session, a meeting of the administration members was held, at which it was determined to renew the gag: and as a proof of the devotion of the democratic party at the North to the cause of slavery, it was arranged that now, for the first time, the odious measure should be proposed by a northern man: nay, not merely a northern man, but a native of New England—a representative from New Hampshire. The resolution was accordingly introduced, and was passed on the 12th December, 1838, and has given notoriety to the name of *Atherton*.

Thus we see a persevering, systematic effort on the part of Congress to protect slavery by suppressing debate, and throwing contempt upon the petitions of hundreds of thousands of American citizens. That this should be done by slaveholders was perhaps to be expected; but that they should be aided in such a desperate assault upon constitutional liberty by northern men, for the paltry consideration of southern votes and southern trade, is mortifying and alarming. The meeting of extremes is a trite illustration of human inconsistency. If in Doctor Johnson's time the loudest yelps for liberty were heard from the drivers of slaves; the loudest yelps in the northern States against aristocracy, chartered monopolies and oppression of the poor, are now heard from men who are laboring to perpetuate the bondage of millions, by gag laws, and restrictions on the freedom of speech and the press. These men are acting from party views, and are rushing to battle under the war cry of " VAN BUREN AND SLAVERY," in hopes, through southern auxiliaries, of enjoying the spoils of victory. Others again, without the slightest sympathy in the political principles of these men, and with their ears stuffed, and their hearts padded with cotton, are co-operating with them in behalf of slavery, from their love of southern trade.* We will here close our protracted investigation with a brief

* The following are strong and amusing instances of the meeting of extremes. In the Spring of 1837, the *whig* merchants of New York, sent a deputation to Washington to request the President to adopt certain measures to relieve the commercial embarrassments of the country. The request was declined, and a great meeting was convened to receive the report of the deputation. The report which was adopted by the meeting, recommended efforts to displace Mr. Van Buren, and as one means of effecting this object, exhorted the merchants to " appeal to our brethren of the South for their generous co-operation ; and *promise* them that those who believe the possession of property of *any* kind " (not excepting men, women, and children,) " is an evidence of merit, will be the last to interfere with the rights of property of *any* kind ; discourage any effort to awaken an excitement, the bare idea of which *should make every husband and father shudder with horror.*" In plain English, if the slaveholders would make common cause with the New York merchants against Mr. Van Buren, they in return would make common cause with the slaveholders against the abolitionists. But democrats know the value of southern votes quite as well as the whigs. Accordingly we find in the Washington Globe of February 9, 1839, a speech *intended* to have been delivered, but prevented by the gag-resolution, by Mr. Eli Moore, a double-refined democrat, President of the New York Trades' Union, and representive from that city in Congress. This gentleman tells us " the wild, enthusiastic, and impetuous spirit which kindled the fires of Smithfield, and strewed the plains of Palestine with the

RECAPITULATION OF THE ACTION OF THE FEDERAL GOVERN-
MENT IN BEHALF OF SLAVERY.

This action we have found exhibited (omitting constitutional provisions)

1. In its appointments to office.
2. In its legislation for Florida.

corses of the crusaders, stands with lighted and uplifted torch hard by the side of abolitionism, ready to spread conflagration and death around the land"— he delares that " so long as the DEMOCRATIC or State Rights' party shall maintain the ascendency, the efforts of the abolitionists will be comparatively innoxious ;" and he announces what will be no less news to the New York merchants, than it is to abolitionists, that " the Federal or NATIONAL BANK PARTY, believe the Federal Legislature not only have the power to abolish slavery in this District of Columbia, *but also in the States.*"

Almost immediately after the publication of this speech, the democratic papers contained the following announcement.—"JUST AND MERITED—the Hon. Eli Moore of the City of New York, has been appointed surveyor of that port." The reward was paid by the President and Senate.

But the most extraordinary instance of the devotion of northern democracy to southern despotism, we have yet met with, was lately given in the City of New York. A set of men, calling themselves " delegates of the *democratic republican party (!!)* for the several wards," assembled to make preparations for commemorating the declaration that " all men are born free and equal." They resolved to have an orator for the occasion ; but so ardent and sublimated was their love of liberty, that no northern democrat was worthy, in their opinion, to declaim before them on the " self eviden truths," and the blessing of the Federal Union. So they selected for their fourth of July orator, JOHN C. CALHOUN, of South Carolina, who had evinced his attachment to the Union by his efforts to excite civil war—to the liberties of his country, by his gag-resolutions, and his bill establishing a censorship of the press—and to the rights of man, by his avowed desire for the everlasting bondage of millions of his fellow men. The presidential election is approaching, the vote of South Carolina is doubtful, and a compliment to Mr. Calhoun, may not be useless to Mr. Van Buren.

3. In its interference in behalf of the slaveholders in Louisiana.

4. In its efforts to degrade the free people of color

5. In its tolerance of slavery in territories under its exclusive jurisdiction.

6. In its arbitrary, unconstitutional, and wicked laws for the arrest of fugitive slaves.

7. In its negotiation with Great Britain and Mexico for the surrender of fugitive slaves.

8. In its invasion of Florida, in pursuit of fugitive slaves.

9. In its negotiations with Great Britain for compensation for slaves who had taken refuge on board British ships of war.

10. In its negotiation with Great Britain for compensation for slaves, ship-wrecked in the West Indies.

11. In its tolerance, protection, and regulation of the American slave trade.

12. In its duplicity, with regard to the abolition of the African slave trade.

13. In its present virtual toleration of the trade.

14. In its appropriations to the Colonization Society.

15. In its Indian treaties in behalf of slaveholders.

16. In its attempted expulsion of the Seminoles for harboring fugitive slaves.

17. In its efforts to prevent the abolition of slavery in Cuba.

18. In its conduct towards Hayti.

19. In its conduct towards Texas.

20. In its attempt to establish a censorship of the press.

21. In its invasion of the right of petition, and the freedom of debate.

Such has been the action in behalf of human bond
age, of a Government which, in the language of the
Constitution, was formed to establish JUSTICE, and
secure the blessings of LIBERTY.

And by whom are the men composing the Government, which thus perverts the objects of its institution, invested with their power? They are the
agents, the mere instruments of the people of the
United States—of the North and the East, as well as
of the West and the South. This consideration calls
us to consider

THE RESPONSIBILITY OF THE FREE STATES.

The advocates of slavery and the tools of party,
are continually telling us, that " *the North has nothing
to do with slavery.*" A volume might be filled with
facts, proving the fallacy of this assertion. There is
scarcely a family among us, that is not connected by
the ties of friendship, kindred, or pecuniary interest,
with the land of slaves. That land is endeared to us
by a thousand recollections—with that land we have
continual commercial, political, religious, and social
intercourse. There, in innumerable instances, are
our personal friends, our brothers, our sons and our
daughters. How malignant and foolish then is the
falsehood, that the thousands and tens of thousands
of abolitionists among us, are anxious to see that land
reeking in blood! But the more intimate are our
connections with that land, the more exposed are we
to be contaminated by its pollutions; and the more
imperatively are we bound to seek its real welfare.

Let it then sink deep in our hearts—let it rest upon

our consciences, that in every wicked and cruel act
of the Federal Government in behalf of slavery, the
people of the North have participated,—we might
almost say that for all this wickedness and cruelty,
they are *solely responsible ;* since it could not have
been perpetrated but with the consent of *their* representatives. Vast and fertile territories, which might
now have been inhabited by a free and happy population, have by northern votes been converted, to use
the language of the poet, into

" A land of tyrants, and a den of slaves."

By northern Senators have our African slavers been
protected from the search of British cruisers. By
northern representatives is the American slave trade
protected, and the abominations enacted in the Capital of the Republic, sanctioned and perpetuated : and
northern men are the officiating ministers in the sacrifice of constitutional liberty on the altar of Moloch.
But representatives are only the agents of their constituents, speaking their thoughts, and doing their
will.   THE PEOPLE OF THE NORTH have done " this
great wickedness."   When *they* repent, when *they*
love mercy, and seek after justice, their representatives will no longer rejoice to aid in transforming the
image of God into a beast of burden—then will the
human shambles be overthrown in the Capital—then
will slavers, " freighted with despair," no longer de-
part from the port of Alexandria, nor chained coffles
traverse the streets of Washington.   Then will the
powers of the Federal Government be exercised in
protecting, not in annihilating the rights of man ; and
then will the slaveholder, deprived of the countenance

of the free States, as he is already of nearly all the rest of the civilized world, be led to reflect calmly on the character and tendency of the institution he now so dearly prizes, and seek his own welfare and that of his children in its voluntary and peaceful abolition.

But here we are confronted with direful prophecies. Let us then proceed to inquire into

THE PROBABLE INFLUENCE OF THE ANTI-SLAVERY AGITATION ON THE PERMANENCY OF THE UNION.

Before we can predict what this influence will be, we must first inquire, what will probably be the direction and aim of the agitation? Every State possesses all the powers of independent sovereignty, except such as she has delegated to the Federal Government. All the powers not specified in the Constitution as delegated, are by that instrument reserved. Among the powers specified, that of abrogating the slave codes of the several States, is not included; on the contrary, the guarantee of the continuance of the African slave trade for twenty years, the provision for the arrest of fugitive slaves, and the establishment of the federal ratio of representation, all refer to and acknowledge the existence of slavery under State authority. If, therefore, the abolitionists, unmindful of their solemn and repeated disclaimers of all power in Congress to legislate for the abolition of slavery in the States, should, with unexampled perfidy, attempt to bring about such legislation—and if Congress, regardless of their oaths, should ever be guilty of the consummate folly and wickedness of passing a law emancipating the slaves held under

State authority, the Union would most unquestionably be rent in twain. The South would indeed be craven could it submit to such profligate usurpation; it would be compelled to withdraw, not for the preservation of slavery alone, but for the protection of all its rights; and indeed the liberties of every State would be jeoparded under a government, which, spurning all constitutional restraints, should assume the omnipotence of the British Parliament. But it is scarcely worth while to anticipate the consequence of an act which can never be perpetrated so long as the people of the North retain an ordinary share of honesty and intelligence.

We have, under all the circumstances of the case, sufficient reasons for believing that the anti-slavery of the North, will carry its action to the very limits of the Constitution, but not beyond them. In despite of the coalitions of parties, and the intrigues of politicians, liberty of speech and of the press will be maintained, and the discussion of slavery will be extended by the very efforts made to arrest it. Let us suppose this discussion to be attended with its natural and probable result, the conversion of the great mass of the northern people to the principles and avowed objects of the abolitionists. Of course, those principles and objects will be embraced by their representatives in Congress. In this case, we may expect that slavery will be abolished in the District of Columbia, and that it will be prohibited in the territories hereafter to be formed on the West of the Mississippi. Thus far the constitutional power of Congress cannot be rationally questioned. Independent of the exclusive jurisdiction over the territories

19

granted to Congress, we have the preceaent of the ordinance of 1787, prohibiting slavery in the North-west Territory, and the more recent precedent of the prohibition of it in the Louisiana territory north of 36½° of north latitude. The American slave trade is now, and has been for upwards of thirty years, pro-hibited in vessels under forty tons burden. It would not be easy to show that the Constitution forbids its prohibition in vessels *over* forty tons burden. We may therefore take it for granted, that the *Senate's coasting trade* will be legally abolished. Should the land traffic not be also destroyed, it would not be for want of disposition, or constitutional power in Con-gress, but on account of the extreme difficulty which would exist in preventing evasions of the law.

We have now the sum total of national legislation, which, on our present supposition, will result from the anti-slavery action at the North. Yet we are posi-tively assured that such legislation would cause a dis-solution of the Union. Now admitting the constitu-tional right, and the moral obligation of our national legislators, to pass the laws in question, it would be difficult to decide by what code of morals they could be excused from the discharge of their duty by the apprehension of consequences. If God governs the world, more is to be feared from rebellion, than from obedience to his will. If his wisdom and goodness are both infinite, his will is and must be an infallible standard of expediency. If it be folly to barter a single soul for the whole world, would it be wise to expose a nation to the wrath of Heaven, for a boon which we now hold, and would continue to hold at the pleasure of men who are daily threatening to deprive us of it?

But we have no fears that Congress will ever find the faithful discharge of their duty, conflicting with the welfare and preservation of the Union. How far selfish and influential individuals may succeed in raising up at the South a party for secession, it is impossible to predict; but it is not difficult to show that a separation founded on the legislation we have specified, would be most preposterous and disastrous, and therefore we may reasonably presume it will not occur.

Should the slave States secede, they would do so, we may suppose, for one or more of the following reasons, viz.

1. To protect their rights from invasion.

2. To guard and perpetuate the institution of slavery.

3. To increase their wealth and power.

The North is the strongest portion of the confederacy; and whenever, unmindful of the federal compact, it wickedly and forcibly usurps power to the prejudice of the South, secession is the only resource left to the latter for the protection of its rights. But a disregard to the *wishes*, does not necessarily imply a violation of the *rights* of the South. Not one of the measures we have contemplated as the probable result of the anti-slavery agitation, encroaches on the constitutional rights of the South; and therefore secession, however it might be professedly justified, would in fact be prompted by other motives than that of self-defence. But so long as the Federal Government confines its action against

slavery within the limits of the Constitution, in
what way would secession tend to guard and perpetuate the institution?

It is natural that the slaveholders should wish to
destroy the influence of the abolitionists, and hence
they have very unjustifiably expressed fears respecting them which they do not feel, and circulated calumnies which they do not believe. The
following admissions reveal the *true* nature of the
apprehensions entertained by the slaveholders.

Mr. CALHOUN, alluding in the Senate to opinions expressed by some of his southern colleagues, exclaimed: " Do they expect the abolitionists will resort to
arms, and commence a crusade to liberate our slaves
by force? Is this what they mean when they speak
of the attempt to abolish slavery? If so, let me tell
our friends of the South who differ from us, that the
war which the abolitionists wage against us, is of a
very different character, and far more effective—it is
waged not against our lives, but our character."

Mr. DUFF GREEN, the editor of the United States
Telegraph, and the great champion of slavery, thus
expressed himself in his paper. " We are of those
who believe the South has nothing to fear from a servile war. We do not believe that the abolitionists *intend*, nor could they if they would, excite the slaves to
insurrection. The danger of this is remote. We
believe that we have most to fear from the organized
action upon the *consciences* and fears of the slaveholders themselves; from the insinuation of their
dangerous heresies into our schools, our pulpits, and
our domestic circles. It is only by *alarming the
consciences* of the weak and feeble, and diffusing

among our people a morbid sensibility on the question of slavery, that the abolitionists can accomplish their object."*

We would now respectfully submit to Mr. Calhoun's consideration, whether a secession would tend in any way to defend the *characters* of slaveholders from the war he contends is waged against them; or fortify their *consciences* against the "dangerous heresies" by which they are assailed?

The new slave nation would acquire from her separate independence, no new power to darken the understandings, or benumb the consciences of her citizens. The freedom of the press throughout the whole slave region, is already extinguished.† Not one single newspaper, from Maryland to Florida, dares to raise its voice in favor of immediate emancipation; and a southern publication, for expressing views unfavorable to slavery, notwithstanding its bitter denunciations of abolitionists, was lately taken from a post-office in Virginia, and in pursuance *of the laws of the State*, committed to the flames by order of the public

* The New York Whig merchants may learn from this candid avowal, that the "bare idea" of the abolition excitement does *not* make every "husband and father shudder with horror" at the South, whatever it may do in Wall street.

† This assertion will not probably be denied, still it may not be amiss to adduce *southern* proof of its truth. *The Missouri Argus*, published at St. Louis, speaking, in April, 1839, of an editor in Ohio, remarked, "Mr. Hammond deems the co-operation of the Eastern fanatics to be all-important to the success of Whiggery, and fears that the timid course of his brother editors on this subject may be productive of mischief. He should recollect, however, that the abolition editors in slave States will not dare to avow their opinions. It would be INSTANT DEATH to them."

19*

authorities; and when the laws are silent, Lynch clubs are ready to visit with infamous and cruel penalties the man who presumes to advocate the inalienable rights of man. What new ramparts could the south-ern confederacy build around their beloved institu-tion? What new weapons could they forge against freedom of discussion?

At the North, the discussion of slavery is now greatly restricted by political and mercenary consid-erations; but such considerations would be dissipated in a moment by secession. The very demagogues who are now fawning upon the slaveholders for their votes, would, when they had no longer votes to bestow, seek popularity in ultra hatred to slavery.

The anti-slavery agitation at the North, is at pre-sent chiefly confined to the religious portion of the community; it would then extend to all classes, and be embittered by national animosity. Slavery would appear more odious and detestable than ever, after having destroyed the fair fabric of American Union, and severed the ties of kindred and of friendship, to rivet more firmly the fetters of the bondman.

The slaveholders are now our fellow countrymen and citizens; they would then be foreigners who had discarded our friendship and connection, that they might trample with more unrestrained violence upon the rights and liberties of their fellow-men. These considerations show that any expectation of extin-guishing or weakening the anti-slavery feeling at the North by separation, must be utterly futile.

A separation would, moreover, deprive the institu-tion of the protection of the Federal Government. Should the slaves attempt to revolt, the masters would be left to struggle with them, unaided by the fleets and armies of the whole Republic.

And by what power would the master recapture his fugitive who had crossed the boundary of the new empire ? Now he may hunt him through the whole confederacy, nor is the trembling wretch secure of his liberty, till he beholds the British standard waving above him. *Then* freedom would be the boon of every slave who could swim the Ohio, or reach the frontier line of the free republic. And this frontier line, be it remembered, *would be continually advancing South.* The anti-slavery feelings of the North, aggravated as they would be by the secession, would afford every possible facility to the fugitive, and laws would then be passed, not for the restoration of human property, but for the protection of human rights.

Would the dissolution of the Union afford the southern planters a more unrestricted enjoyment of the foreign or domestic slave trade ? Alas ! from the moment of separation, slave trading becomes PIRACY in fact, as well as in name, and the crews of New Orleans and Alexandria, as well as of African slavers, would swing on northern gibbets.

We confess then our utter inability to perceive in what possible mode, a secession of the southern States would tend to guard and perpetuate the institution of slavery.

Would a dissolution of the Union augment the power and wealth of the slave States ? The power and wealth of a nation depend on its population, industry, and commerce. The increase of the white population at the South is now small, compared with the wonderful tide of life which is rolling over the

western plains.   And when the southern region shall
be insulated from the sympathies of the whole civilized world, and consecrated to a stern and remorseless
despotism,—a despotism sooner or later to be engulfed
in blood, by what attraction will it divert the tide of
emigration from the fair prairies of the west, to its
own sugar and cotton-fields ? If, even now, armed
patroles must traverse at night the streets and high-
ways that the whites may sleep in safety, and military
preparation is essential to domestic security,* what
husband or father will take up his residence in the
new empire when withdrawn from the protection of
the Federal Government, and the friendship of its
neighbors ? The slaves are now rapidly gaining on
their masters, and will increase in a still greater ratio
after the separation, since the prudent and the enterprising will abandon the doomed region, and few or
none will enter it from without.   Hence it is obvious
that the white population of the southern States could
gain no accession from their erection into a separate
confederacy.

Would secession augment the wealth of the South ?
Be it remembered that there is now no one restriction on southern industry and enterprise which separation would remove.   The slaveholders in Congress
with rare exceptions, have conducted the affairs of
the nation to suit themselves.   So far as the interests
of the northern manufacturer were identified with the

* " A state of military preparation must always be with us a
state of perfect domestic security.   A profound peace, and consequent apathy, may expose us to the danger of domestic insurrection."—*Message of Gov. Hayne to the Legislature of South Carolina,* 1833.

tariff, they have been sacrificed at the mandate of the cotton grower ; and so far as national legislation can promote the wealth of the South, the statutes are already enacted.

It will not be denied that the larger portion of the strength of the Union—population, money, commerce, and shipping is to be found at the North. In all these elements of national power, the South participates equally with the North. The foreign invader is kept from her shores, and her property abroad is protected from spoliation at least as much by the power of the North as by her own. Her strength for all purposes of defence, is the strength of the Union. What would it be after secession ? True it is, the South would receive Texas into her arms, but she would derive neither honor nor power from the loathsome embrace. Annexation *now* would ensure to her the political dominion of the whole Republic, but *after* secession, would cause rather weakness than strength.

As we can discover no possible advantage which the South could derive from secession, we are convinced that the threats of dissolving the Union, which her statesmen are so prodigal in scattering, are the ebullitions of passion, or the devices of policy, rather than the result of mature determination. This conviction is strengthened by still further considerations.

Should the slave States withdraw without any aggression on their rights, but for the sole purpose of enjoying in greater privacy and tranquillity the sweets of slavery, they would leave the whole North in a state of high exasperation. The ligaments which have so long bound us together, cannot be ruthlessly and wantonly torn asunder, without causing deep and festering wounds, the consequences of which, the imagination revolts from anticipating. And in what light would the dark and gloomy despotism be viewed by the civilized world? Mankind would behold, and wonder, and despise. The new State would be excluded from the companionship of nations. Her cotton would indeed be still purchased, as we buy the coffee of Hayti; but with the least possible intimacy. Already is our Minister at London treated with contumely, because he is a slaveholder—as the representative only of the men who had shattered the American Republic to secure the permanency of human bondage, he would not be endured at any court in Europe with the exception of Constantinople In a few years, the slaves would attain a frightful numerical superiority over their masters. The dread of insurrection within, and of aggression from without, would realize the prediction of holy writ, when men's hearts shall fail them for fear, and for looking after those things which are coming on the earth. At length the fatal period would arrive, when, stung with insults and injuries, the new empire would appeal to arms; and should a hostile army land upon its shores, the standard of emancipation would be reared, and slavery would expire in blood.*

* " March 29, 1779. The committee appointed to take into consideration the circumstances of the *southern* states, and the ways and means for their safety and defence, report—That the State of South Carolina, as represented by the delegates of the said State, and by Mr. Huger, who has come hither at the request of the governor of said State, on purpose to explain the particular circumstances thereof, *is unable to make any effectual efforts with*

We well know with what indignant feelings these
pages will at first be read by many; and fortunate
shall we deem ourselves should we escape the imputation of writing to promote insurrection and disunion. But we appeal from the decision of angry
passion, to that of calm reflection. Do we not speak
the words of truth and soberness? Do not the signs
of the times warrant our predictions? In what respect do the sentiments we have uttered conflict with
the lessons of history, or the character of human nature? Do we love the union of the States? (!) If
such a love can descend by inheritance, we should
possess it; if it can be founded on the most thorough
conviction of the importance of union not merely to
the prosperity of our country, but to the happiness of
numerous and beloved children and relatives, we
should possess it. If the history of the States of
Greece, of Italy, of Holland, of Germany, of South
America, and of our own land, demonstrates the blessings of union, and the calamities of separation; then
should the prayer of every American ascend to Heaven for the perpetuity of the American Union. But
let it be a union for the preservation, not the destruc-

*militia, by reason of the great proportion of citizens necessary to
remain at home to prevent insurrection among the negroes, and to
prevent the desertion of them to the enemy.* That the state of the
country and the *great numbers* of those people among them, expose
the inhabitants *to great danger* from the endeavors of the enemy
to excite them either to revolt or desert."—*Secret Journal of Congress,* vol. i. p. 105.

Whether the South Carolinians are from their present "particular circumstances," less in danger from a foreign invader than in
1779, may be seen from the following statement:—in 1790 there
were in that state 107,094 slaves and 140,178 whites; in 1830, the
colored population was 323,322, the white only 257,863.

tion of liberty : a union cemented by a sacred observance of the constitutional compact ; .not enforced by gag laws, a censorship of the press, and the abrogation of the right of petition—a union in conformity with the will of God, not in contempt of his authority —a union that shall be regarded as a common blessing, not held as a boon from the South, ever ready to be withdrawn as a penalty for the discharge of moral and political duties.

May Almighty God in mercy preserve the friends of emancipation, from the sin and folly of even hazarding the Union, by the slightest encroachment on the constitutional rights of the South, and may He give them grace to maintain their own rights in defiance of every menace.

APPENDIX.

———

HAVING mentioned the charge made by President Jackson against the New York abolitionists, in his message to Congress, and alluded to the letter they addressed to him respecting it, we have thought it might be useful to insert here the letter itself, as showing more in detail one of the unwarrantable expedients to which the Federal Government has resorted in behalf of slavery.

" *To the President of the United States:*

" SIR :—In your message to Congress of the 7th instant, are the following passages : '1 must also invite your attention to the painful excitement produced in the South, by attempts to circulate through the mails, inflammatory appeals, *addressed to the passions of the slaves,* in prints and in various sorts of publications, *calculated to stimulate them to insurrection, and produce all the horrors of a servile war.* There is, doubtless, no respectable portion of our countrymen who can be so far misled as to feel any other sentiment than that of indignant regret, at conduct so destructive of the harmony and peace of the country, and *so repugnant to the principles of our national compact, and to the dictates of humanity and religion.*' You remark, that it is fortunate that the people of the North have 'given so strong and impressive a tone to the sentiments entertained against the proceedings of the misguided persons who have engaged in these *unconstitutional and wicked attempts.*' And you proceed to sug-

20

gest to Congress, 'the propriety of passing such a law as will prohibit, under severe penalties, the circulation in the southern States, through the mails, of incendiary publications, *intended to instigate the slaves to insurrection.*'

"A servile insurrection, as experience has shown, involves the slaughter of the whites, -without respect to sex or age. Hence, sir, the purport of the information you have communicated to Congress and to the world, is, that there are American citizens who, in violation of the dictates of humanity and religion, have engaged in unconstitutional and wicked attempts to circulate, through the mails, inflammatory appeals addressed to the passions of the slaves, and which appeals, as is implied in the object of your proposed law, are *intended* to stimulate the slaves to indiscriminate massacre. Recent events irresistibly confine the application of your remarks to the officers and members of the American Anti-slavery Society and its auxiliaries.

"On the 28th of March, 1834, the Senate of the United States passed the following resolution :

'Resolved, That the President, in relation to the public revenue, has assumed upon himself authority and power not conferred by the Constitution and laws, but in derogation of both.'

"On the 5th of the ensuing month, you transmitted to that body your 'solemn protest' against their decision. Instructed by your example, we now, sir, in behalf of the Society of which we are the constituted organs, and in behalf of all who are associated with it, present to you this, our 'solemn protest,' against your grievous and unfounded accusations.

"Should it be supposed, that in thus addressing you, we are wanting in the respect due to your exalted station, we offer, in our vindication, your own acknowledgement to the Senate : 'Subject only to the restraints of truth and justice, the free people of the United States have the undoubted right as individuals, or collectively, orally, or in writing, at such times and in such language and form as they may think proper, to discuss his (the President's) official conduct, and to express and promulgate their opinions concerning it.'

"In the exercise of this 'undoubted right,' we protest against the judgment you have pronounced against the abolitionists.

"*First.* Because, in rendering that judgment officially, you assumed a power not belonging to your office.

"You complained that the resolution censuring your conduct, 'though adopted by the Senate in its legislative capacity, is, in its effects and in its characteristics, essentially *judicial.*' And thus, sir, although the charges of which we complain were made by you in your executive capacity, they are, equally with the resolution, essentially *judicial.* The Senate adjudged that your conduct was unconstitutional. You pass the same judgment on our efforts. Nay, sir, you go farther than the Senate. That body forebore to impeach your motives—but you have assumed the prerogatives, not only of a court of law, but of conscience—and pronounce our efforts to be *wicked* as well as unconstitutional.

"*Secondly.* We protest against the *publicity* you have given to your accusations.

"You felt it to be a grievance, that the charge against you was 'spread upon the Journal of the Senate, published to the nation and to the world—made part of our enduring archives, and incorporated in the history of the age. The punishment of removal from office, and future disqualification, does not follow the decision; but the *moral influence* of a solemn declaration by a majority of the Senate, that the accused is guilty of the offence charged upon him, has been as effectually secured as if the like declaration had been made upon an impeachment expressed in the same terms.'

"And is it nothing, sir, that we are officially charged by the President of the United States, with wicked and unconstitutional efforts, and with harboring the most execrable intentions; and, this too, in a document spread upon the Journals of both Houses of Congress, published to the nation and to the world, made part of our enduring archives, and incorporated in the history of the age? It is true, that although you have given judgment against us, you cannot award execution. We are not, indeed, subjected to the penalty of murder; but need we ask you, sir, what must be the *moral influence* of your declaration, that we have intended its perpetration ?

" *Thirdly.* We protest against your condemnation of us *unheard.*

" What, sir, was your complaint against the Senate ? ' Without notice, *unheard,* and untried, I find myself charged, on the records of the Senate, and in a form unknown in our country, with the high crime of violating the laws and Constitution of my country. No notice of the charge was given to the accused, and no opportunity afforded him to respond to the accusation—to meet his accusers face to face—to cross-examine the witnesses—to procure counteracting testimony, or to be heard in in his defence.'

" Had you, sir, done to others, as it thus seems you would that others should do to you, no occasion would have been given for this protest. You most truly assert, in relation to the conduct of the Senate, ' It is the policy of our benign system of jurisprudence, to secure in all criminal proceedings, and even in the most trivial litigations, a fair, unprejudiced, and impartial trial.' And by what authority, sir, do you except such of your fellow-citizens as are known as abolitionists, from the benefit of this benign system ? When has a fair, unprejudiced, and impartial trial been accorded to those who dare to maintain that all men are equally entitled to life, liberty, and the pursuit of happiness ? What was the trial, sir, which preceded the judgment you have rendered against them ?

" *Fourthly.* We protest against the *vagueness* of your charges.

" We cannot more forcibly describe the injustice you have done us than by adopting your own indignant remonstrance, against what you deemed similar injustice on the part of the Senate : ' Some of the first principles of natural right and enlightened jurisprudence, have been violated in the very form of the resolution. It carefully abstains from averring in *which* of the late proceedings the President has assumed upon himself authority and power not conferred by the Constitution and laws. Why was not the certainty of the offence, the nature and cause of the accusation, set out in the manner required in the Constitution, before even the humblest individual, for the smallest crime, can be exposed to condemnation? Such a specification was due to the accused, that he might direct his defence to the real points of attack. A more striking illustration of the soundness and necessity of the rules which forbid *vague and indefinite general-ities,* and require a reasonable certainty in all judicial allegations, and a more glaring instance of the violation of these rules, has seldom been exhibited.'

" It has been reserved for you, sir, to exhibit a still more strik-ing illustration of the importance of these rules, and a still more glaring instance of their violation. You have accused an inde-finite number of your fellow citizens, without designation of name or residence, of making unconstitutional and wicked ef-forts, and of harboring intentions which could be entertained only by the most depraved and abandoned of mankind; and yet you carefully abstain from averring *which* article of the Constitu-tion they have transgressed; you omit stating when, where, and by whom these wicked attempts were made; you give no specification of the inflammatory appeals which you assert have been addressed to the passions of the slaves. You well know that the *'moral influence'* of your charges will affect thousands of your countrymen, many of them your political friends—some of them heretofore honored with your confidence—most, if not all of them, of irreproachable characters; and yet, by the very vagueness of your charges, you incapacitate each one of this multitude from proving his innocence.

" *Fifthly.* We protest against your charges, because they are *untrue.* Surely, sir, the burthen of proof rests upon you. If you possess evidence against us, we are by your own showing, entitled to 'an opportunity to cross-examine witnesses, to pro-cure counteracting testimony, and to be heard in [*our*] defence.' You complained that you had been denied such an opportunity. It was not to have been expected, then, that you would make the conduct of the Senate the model of your own. Conscious of the wrong done to you, and protesting against it, you found yourself compelled to enter on your defence. You have placed

20*

us in similar circumstances, and we proceed to follow your example :

" The substance of your various allegations may be embodied in the charge, that *we have attempted to circulate, through the mails, appeals addressed to the passions of the slaves, calculated to stimulate them to insurrection, and with the intention of producing a servile war.*

" It is deserving of notice, that the *attempt* to circulate our papers, is alone charged upon us. It is not pretended that we have put our appeals into the hands of a single slave, or that, in any instance, our endeavors to excite a servile war have been crowned with success. And in what way was our most execrable attempts made ? By secret agents, traversing the slave country in disguise, stealing by night into the hut of the slave, and there reading to him our inflammatory appeals ? You, sir, answer this question by declaring, that we attempted the mighty mischief by circulating our appeals ' THROUGH THE MAILS !' And are the southern slaves, sir, accustomed to receive periodicals by mail ? Of the thousands of publications mailed from the Anti-slavery office for the South, did you ever hear, sir, of one solitary paper being addressed to a slave ? Would you know to whom they were directed, consult the southern newspapers, and you will find them complaining that they were sent to public officers, clergymen, and other influential citizens. Thus it seems we are incendiaries, who place the torch in the hands of him whose dwellings we would fire ! We are conspiring to excite a servile war, and announce our design to the masters, and commit to their care and disposal the very instruments by which we expect to effect our purpose ! It has been said that thirty or forty of our papers were received at the South, directed to free people of color. We cannot deny the assertion, because these papers may have been mailed by others, for the sinister purpose of charging the act upon us. We are, however, ready to make our several affidavits, that not one paper, with our knowledge, or by our authority, has ever been sent to any such person in a slave State. The free people of color at the South can exert no influence in behalf of the enslaved ; and we have no disposition to excite odium against them, by making them the recipients of our publications.

" Your proposal that a law should be passed, punishing the circulation, through the mails, of papers *intended to excite the slaves to insurrection,* necessarily implies that such papers are now circulated ; and you expressly and positively assert, that we have attempted to circulate appeals addressed to the passions of the slaves, and *calculated to produce all the horrors of a servile war.* We trust, sir, your proposed law, so portentous to the freedom of the press, will not be enacted, till you have furnished Congress with stronger evidence of its necessity than unsupported / assertions. We hope you will lay before that body, for its information, the papers to which you refer. This is the more necessary, as the various public journals and meetings which have denounced us for entertaining insurrectionary and murderous designs, have in no instance been able to quote from our publications, a single exhortation to the slaves to break their fetters, or the expression of a solitary wish for a servile war.

" How far our writings are *'calculated'* to produce insurrection, is a question which will be variously decided according to the latitude in which it is discussed. When we recollect that the humble school-book, the tale of fiction, and the costly annual have been placed under the ban of southern editors for trivial allusions to slavery—and that a southern divine has warned his fellow-citizens of the danger of permitting slaves to be present at the celebration of our national festival, where they might, listen to the Declaration of Independence, and to eulogiums on liberty,—we have little hope that our disquisitions on human rights will be generally deemed safe and innocent, where those rights are habitually violated. Certain writings of one of your predecessors, President Jefferson, would undoubtedly be regarded, in some places, so insurrectionary as to expose to popular violence whoever should presume to circulate them.

" As therefore, sir, there is no common standard by which the criminality of opinions respecting slavery can be tested, we acknowledge the foresight which prompted you to recommend, that the 'severe penalties' of your proposed law should be awarded, not according to the character of the publication, but the *intention* of the writer. Still, sir, we apprehend that no trivial difficulties will be experienced in the application of your law. The writer may be anonymous, or beyond the reach of prosecution, while the porter who deposites the papers in the post-office, and the mail carrier who transports them, having no evil intentions, cannot be visited with the 'severe penalties;' and thus will your law fail in securing to the South that entire exemption from all discussion on the subject of slavery, which it so vehemently desires. The success of the attempt already made to establish a censorship of the press, is not such as to invite farther encroachment on the rights of the people to publish their sentiments.

"In your protest, you remarked to the Senate: 'The whole Executive power being vested in the President, who is *responsible* for its exercise, it is a necessary consequence that he should have a right to employ agents of his *own choice*, to aid him in the performance of his duties, and to *discharge* them when he is no longer *willing* to be RESPONSIBLE for their acts. He is equally bound to take care that the laws be faithfully executed, whether they impose duties on the highest officer of State, or the *lowest subordinates* in any of the departments.'

"It may not be uninteresting to you, sir, to be informed in what manner your 'Subordinate' in New York, who, on your 'responsibility,' is exercising the functions of Censor of the American press, discharges the arduous duties of this untried, and until now, unheard of office. We beg leave to assure you, that his task is executed with a simplicity of principle, and celerity of despatch, unknown to any Censor of the press in France or Austria. Your subordinate decides upon the incendiary character of the publications committed to the post-office, by a glance at the wrappers or bags in which they are contained. No packages sent to be mailed from our office, and directed to a slave State, can escape the vigilance of this inspector of canvass and brown paper. Even your own protest, sir, if in an anti-slavery envelope, would be arrested on its progress to the South, as 'inflammatory, incendiary, and insurrectionary in the highest degree.'

" No veto, however, is *as yet* imposed on the circulation of publications from any printing-office but our own. Hence, when we desire to send 'appeals' to the South, all that is necessary is, to insert them in some newspaper that espouses our principles, pay for as many thousand copies as we think proper, and order them to be mailed according to our instructions.

" Such, sir, is the worthless protection purchased for the South, by the most unblushing and dangerous usurpation of which any public officer has been guilty since the organization of our Federal Government. Were the Senate, in reference to your acknowledged responsibility for the conduct of your subordinates, to resolve ' that the President, in relation to the suppression of certain papers in the New York Post Office, has assumed upon himself authority and power not conferred by the Constitution and laws, but in derogation of both ;' instead of protesting against the charge, you would be compelled to acknowledge its truth, and you would plead the *necessity* of the case in your vindication. The weight to be attached to such a plea, may be learned from the absurdity and inefficacy of the New York Censorship. Be assured, sir, your proposed law to punish the *intentions* of an author, will, in its practical operations, prove equally impotent.

" And now, sir, permit us respectfully to suggest to you, the propriety of ascertaining the *real* designs of abolitionists, before your apprehensions of them lead you to sanction any more trifling with the LIBERTY OF THE PRESS. You assume it as a fact, that abolitionists are miscreants, who are laboring to effect the massacre of their southern brethren. Are you aware of the extent of the reproach which such an assumption casts upon the character of your countrymen? In August last, the number of Anti-slavery Societies known to us was 263 ; we have *now* the names of more than 350 societies, and accessions are daily made to the multitude who embrace our principles. And can you think it possible, sir, that these citizens are deliberately plotting murder, and furnishing us with funds to send publications to the South 'intended to instigate the slaves to insurrection ?' Is there any thing in the character and manners of the free States, to warrant the imputation on their citizens of such enormous wickedness? Have you ever heard, sir, of whole communities in these States subjecting obnoxious individuals to a mock trial, and then, in contempt of law, humanity, and religion, deliberately murdering them? You have seen, in the public journals, great rewards offered for the perpetration of horrible crimes. We appeal to your candor, and ask, were these rewards offered by abolitionists, or by men whose charges against abolitionists you have condescended to sanction and disseminate?

"And what, sir, is the character of those whom you have in your message held up to the execration of the civilized world? Their enemies being judges, they are *religious* fanatics. And what are the haunts of these plotters of murder? The pulpit, the bench, the bar, the professor's chair, the hall of legislation the meeting for prayer, the temple of the Most High. But strange and monstrous as is this conspiracy, still you believe in its existence, and call on Congress to counteract it. Be persuaded, sir, the moral sense of the community is abundantly sufficient to render this conspiracy utterly impotent the moment its machinations are exposed. Only PROVE the assertions and insinuations in your message, and you dissolve in an instant every Anti-slavery Society in our land. Think not, sir, that we shall interpose any obstacle to an inquiry into our conduct. We invite, nay, sir, we entreat the appointment by Congress of a Committee of Investigation to visit the Anti-slavery Office in New York. They shall be put in possession of copies of all the publications that have been issued from our press. Our whole correspondence shall be submitted to their inspection; our accounts of receipts and expenditures shall be spread before them, and we ourselves will cheerfully answer under oath whatever interrogatories they may put to us relating to the charges you have advanced.

"Should such a committee be denied, and should the law you propose, stigmatizing us as felons, be passed without inquiry into the truth of your accusation, and without allowing us a hearing, then shall we make the language of your protest our own, and declare that, ' If such proceedings shall be approved and sustained by an intelligent people, then will the great contest with arbitrary power which had established in statutes, in bills of rights, in sacred charters, and in constitutions of government, the right of every citizen to a notice before trial, to a hearing before condemnation, and to an impartial tribunal for deciding on the charge, have been made in VAIN.'

" Before we conclude, permit us, sir, to offer you the following assurances.

" Our principles, our objects, and our measures, are wholly uncontaminated by considerations of party policy. Whatever may be our respective opinions as citizens, of men and measures, as abolitionists we have expressed no political preferences, and are pursuing no party ends. From neither of the gentlemen nominated to succeed you, have we any thing to hope or fear ; and to neither of them do we intend as abolitionists, to afford any aid or influence. This declaration will, it is hoped, satisfy the partizans of the rival candidates, that it is not necessary for them to assail our rights by way of convincing the South that they do not possess our favor.

" We have addressed you, sir, on this occasion, with republican plainness, and Christian sincerity ; but with no desire to derogate from the respect that is due to you, or wantonly to give you pain. To repel your charges, and to disabuse the public, was a duty we owed to ourselves, to our chileren, and above all to the great and holy cause in which we are engaged. That cause we believe is approved by our Maker; and while we retain this belief, it is our intention, trusting to His direction and protection, to persevere in our endeavors to impress upon the minds and hearts of our countrymen, the sinfulness of claiming property in human beings, and the duty and wisdom of immediately relinquishing it.

" When convinced that our endeavors are wrong, we shall abandon them ; but such conviction must be produced by other arguments than vituperation, popular violence, or penal enactments.

ARTHUR TAPPAN,
WILLIAM JAY,
JOHN RANKIN,
ABRAHAM L. COX,
JOSHUA LEAVITT,
SIMEON S. JOSELYN,
LEWIS TAPPAN,
THEODORE S. WRIGHT,
SAMUEL E. CORNISH,
ELIZUR WRIGHT, JR.

Executive Committee.

NEW YORK, Dec. 26, 1835.